WEALTH CONNECTION with NATURE

HARISH CHANDRA KALRA

ISBN 979-8-89777-910-9

"Thank You, O Divine"

Thank you, O God, for the sun and rain,

For rivers, forests, and fields of grain.

You nourish all life with love so deep,

Blessing nature and wealth for us to keep.

Dedicated to

My beloved Mother

Late Smt Pushpa Rani Kalra

&

My Hard working Father

Shri Somnath Kalra

Wealth and Nature: A Timeless Tie

In nature's arms, wealth takes its cue,

Sow the right seeds, watch fortunes accrue.

Like rivers fed by waterfalls grand,

Multiple incomes help wealth expand.

Seasons teach patience, cycles unfold,

History repeats, as stories are told.

Climb like Everest, steady and wise,

With mentors' vision, reach for the skies.

Earn, protect, and cherish with grace,

Before wealth fades—enjoy its embrace

Contents

Acknowledgement

With a heart full of gratitude, I bow to the Almighty for blessing me with challenges that shaped my journey and for granting me the strength, wisdom, and resilience to overcome them. Every struggle has been a lesson, and every victory, a testament to divine grace.

I extend my deepest gratitude to my father, Mr. Somnath Kalra, whose guidance has been my compass, and to my late mother, Mrs. Pushparani Kalra, whose love and blessings continue to light my path. My heartfelt thanks to my wife, Pooja, for being my unwavering pillar of support, and to my daughter, Avani, whose innocence and love inspire me daily. My sisters, Shilpa and Poonam, have stood by me with unconditional love, offering their time, wisdom, and encouragement during life's most crucial moments—I am forever grateful.

This book would not have been possible without my source of inspiration, especially Team and Members in NJ India Invest Pvt. Ltd., Mutual Fund Distributor Association Bhopal, all Mutual Fund AMCs, and other Mutual Fund Distributor Associations and Insurance companies that have invited me to countless seminars and knowledge sessions. Their trust and platform provided me with invaluable learning experiences, igniting the spark that led to this book.

I also express my sincere thanks to my ex-colleagues from various companies and banks and my current team in my company. Their collaboration, dedication, and support have been instrumental in making this endeavor a reality.

A special note of gratitude to my clients, who are more than just clients — they are my extended family. Through them, I have learned a thousand lessons, gained new perspectives, and discovered the true essence of relationships and trust. Their patience, understanding, and cooperation, especially in challenging times, are beyond words.

I also thank my relatives, neighbor's and friends for their unwavering love and support, especially during difficult times. Their presence has been a source of comfort and strength, making every obstacle easier to overcome.

As I reflect on this journey, I realize that this entire universe has been helping me in one way or another. From people to experiences, from struggles to successes — everything has been divinely orchestrated. Thank you, God, for creating this beautiful universe and for making me a part of it.

With heartfelt gratitude,

– Harish Kalra

To Whom This Book Is Beneficial

The book *"Wealth Connection with Nature"* is crafted with the intention to benefit people across all generations, genders, professions, and walks of life. The core idea of this book revolves around drawing deep inspiration from nature and relating its principles directly and indirectly to wealth creation, accumulation, and management. Nature has always been a guiding force in our lives, and through this book, an attempt has been made to showcase how its principles can effectively transform one's approach toward wealth.

This book is equally beneficial for men and women, irrespective of their age, as the fundamentals of wealth management and creation remain universal. Young individuals who are in the initial stages of their career can draw lessons on how starting early with a small contribution can yield remarkable financial growth over time, similar to how a small seed gradually grows into a gigantic tree with consistent nurturing. On the other hand, individuals who are in their middle or later stages of life can find value in understanding how wealth, if not managed or utilized properly, can lead to loss or stagnation – much like overgrown branches of a tree blocking its growth or withering away due to lack of care.

Whether you are an employee, businessperson, entrepreneur, professional, or freelancer, this book offers insights that can help you enhance your financial knowledge and decision-making skills. Employees may find it useful to learn about consistent savings, systematic investments, and the power of compounding, much like the seasonal changes that gradually lead to bountiful harvests. Businesspersons and entrepreneurs, on the other hand, can relate to nature's principle of expansion and growth, where patience, strategy, and adaptation are the keys to sustainable financial success.

This book also highlights the importance of financial protection, comparing it to nature's defense mechanism. Just as a tree protects itself with strong roots and thick bark, individuals must also protect their wealth through proper financial planning, insurance, and risk management. Readers from any profession can find valuable insights on how to balance income, expenses, savings, and investments — resembling the balanced ecosystem in nature where everything plays a vital role in sustaining life.

Furthermore, this book is for anyone who desires to create and preserve wealth while maintaining a natural balance in life. The lessons drawn from nature will inspire readers to take mindful actions toward wealth creation, utilization, and preservation. Whether you are planning for your future, securing your family's financial well-being, or seeking financial independence, this book serves as a practical guide by connecting natural principles to wealth management strategies.

In essence, *"Wealth Connection with Nature"* is beneficial for everyone — young or old, male or female, salaried or self-employed, experienced or beginner — who seeks to build a sustainable and growing wealth while learning from the vast and insightful principles of nature. Just as nature effortlessly manages growth, balance, and renewal, this book will guide you to adopt the same approach in managing your financial journey.

CHAPTER 1

Sow Seeds of Fruit-Giving Trees for Longer Years

Nature has always been the greatest teacher, showing us the power of patience, care, and long-term rewards. Trees not only clean the air, provide oxygen, and enrich the environment, but certain fruit-bearing trees also offer sustenance and medicinal value for generations. Some of these trees live for centuries, giving continuous returns with minimal care after maturity. Just like wealth, trees require the right selection, nurturing, and patience before they start rewarding us.

Let's explore a few such trees that give fruits for longer years and see what lessons they hold for wealth creation.

1. Olive Tree – A Timeless Provider of Wealth

The olive tree is a symbol of resilience, longevity, and prosperity. It can live for over 500 years, with some trees producing olives for more than 1,000 years. The tree starts yielding fruits in 3-5 years, and with proper care, it continues to provide valuable olives, which are primarily used for oil production.

Olive oil is a high-value commodity in global markets, making olive farming extremely profitable.

These trees thrive even in tough conditions like drought and salinity, demonstrating their strength.

A single adult olive tree produces enough oxygen for four people, contributing to environmental sustainability.

Wealth Lesson: Investments in stable, long-term assets—like real estate, stocks of strong companies, or retirement funds—can provide sustained returns over generations, just like an olive tree bearing fruit for centuries.

2. Pomegranate Tree – The Wealth of Health and Longevity

The pomegranate tree lives for 50+ years, beginning to bear fruit in 3-5 years. Known for its antioxidant-rich fruits, pomegranates have immense medicinal and commercial value.

It contains polyphenols that combat oxidative stress and aging, making it a sought-after health product.

Pomegranate extracts have anti-inflammatory and antimicrobial properties, boosting immunity.

Its farming is highly profitable due to growing demand for health-conscious products.

Wealth Lesson: Just like the pomegranate tree, certain investments (such as health insurance, SIPs, and compounding investments) may seem slow at first, but they provide stability, protection, and long-term financial well-being.

3. Mango Tree – The Sweet Reward of Patience

Mango trees, beloved worldwide, live for 40-100 years and start bearing fruit within 3-6 years. The demand for mangoes remains high, making mango farming a lucrative business.

A mango tree contributes significantly to oxygen production, helping sustain life.

In India, mango trees hold cultural and spiritual significance, often planted in home gardens.

With different varieties ripening at different times, mangoes provide a continuous stream of returns.

Wealth Lesson: Just as mango trees require different climates and conditions to flourish, wealth creation requires diversification— investing in various asset classes like equity funds, bonds, gold, and real estate to ensure consistent financial growth.

4. Mulberry Tree – Small but Steady Growth

The mulberry tree lives for 30-50 years and begins yielding fruit within 3-4 years. Apart from its delicious berries, it plays a crucial role in silkworm farming, making it economically significant.

Mulberry leaves are used in traditional medicine for diabetes and other health benefits.

It is a fast-growing and hardy tree that adapts to different environments easily.

Mulberry farming contributes to the silk industry, demonstrating how indirect benefits can enhance wealth.

Wealth Lesson: Investing in productive assets — such as dividend stocks or dividend yield funds, rental properties, or business ventures — ensures steady income streams over time. Even small but consistent investments can create significant wealth in the long run.

Wealth Connection – Lessons from Long-Living Trees

Observing these long-living, fruit-bearing trees teaches us a crucial wealth-building lesson: growth takes time, care, and the right environment. Just as trees need initial care before becoming self-sustaining, wealth accumulation requires early investments, patience, and proper financial planning.

Long-term Investments Pay Off: Like trees that give fruits for decades, investments in real estate, retirement funds, and equity markets yield the best results when given time.

Patience is Key: Just as trees do not bear fruit immediately, financial assets need time to grow. Wealth creation is a marathon, not a sprint.

Regular Care Ensures Continuous Benefits: Trees need watering, pruning, and pest control—just as investments need monitoring, adjustments, and diversification.

Think Beyond Immediate Gains: Like trees that provide oxygen, shade, and beauty beyond just fruits, wealth should be built not only for personal use but also for family, society, and future generations.

Key Takeaways from This Chapter:

1. Sow the Seeds of Wealth Early: Just as trees must be planted in the right conditions, start your wealth journey with strategic financial planning.

2. Select the Right Investment (Tree) for Your Goals: Different trees have different lifespans and benefits—similarly, choose assets that match your financial goals and time horizon.

3. Care for Your Wealth Like a Living Organism: Regular monitoring, rebalancing, and protecting investments from risks ensure long-term prosperity.

4. Let Wealth Accumulate Before Enjoying the Fruits: Allow investments to mature before withdrawing returns, maximizing compounding benefits.

5. Think Wealth, Grow Wealth, Manage Wealth, and Enjoy Wealth: True financial success comes from not just accumulation but also proper utilization of wealth.

By following nature's wisdom, we can learn to build, nurture, and enjoy wealth that lasts for generations — just like these incredible fruit-giving trees.

The Giving Tree and Wealth

A tree gives fruit, so rich, so sweet,

Yet keeps its roots strong and deep.

Assets, like fruit, must flow and grow,

Not locked away, but shared to show.

Knowledge, kindness, wealth, and time,

When given well, they truly shine.

Give with joy, and watch them rise,

Fortune returns in a sweet surprise!

CHAPTER 2

The Silent Giants and the Art of Wealth Creation

In the heart of ancient forests, towering trees stand as silent witnesses to the passage of time. These giants, some reaching hundreds of feet into the sky, did not emerge overnight. They began as fragile seeds, barely visible to the eye. Their journey to greatness is a slow and steady one, shaped by the unseen forces of nature.

The Growth of a Giant

A tree's growth begins with a single seed finding fertile ground. It does not grow instantly but instead spends its early years establishing strong roots. These roots, hidden beneath the surface, seek out water and nutrients, anchoring the tree against storms and harsh conditions. The deeper and wider the roots spread, the more stability and nourishment the tree gains.

As the years pass, the tree thickens its trunk, strengthening its core to support its expanding branches. Each ring in its trunk tells a story of struggle and survival—droughts, storms, and seasons of abundance. With each passing season, the tree grows taller and stronger, reaching for sunlight, constantly adapting and expanding.

But the secret to its towering presence lies not just in rapid growth but in patience and resilience. A tree does not rush to become a giant; instead, it consistently nurtures itself, ensuring steady progress. This is nature's way—long-term investment, unwavering persistence, and strategic growth.

Wealth Creation: A Similar Journey

Much like trees, wealth does not materialize overnight. It begins with a single financial seed—an idea, a small investment, or a humble beginning. At first, the returns may seem insignificant, much like a sapling barely taller than the grass around it. But the key lies in consistency and nurturing.

Financial roots must be planted—knowledge, discipline, and smart decision-making form the foundation. Just as a tree weathers storms, wealth creation faces its share of market downturns, unexpected expenses, and economic shifts. Those who panic and uproot their investments at the first sign of difficulty never allow them to grow into something substantial.

Over time, small but steady efforts—consistent savings, strategic investments, and reinvesting profits—compound into significant growth.

The longer wealth remains invested, the stronger its foundation becomes. Much like the rings of a tree, each financial decision adds layers of strength to the wealth-building process.

The Power of Time and Patience

Both trees and wealth demand one essential ingredient: time. The most magnificent trees are those that have stood the test of time, weathering adversity while steadily growing. Similarly, the wealthiest individuals are those who understand that financial growth is not a sprint but a marathon.

Patience, resilience, and strategic nurturing lead to financial independence, just as they lead to towering forests. Just as a tree's branches provide shade to those who come after, wealth, when properly cultivated, creates a legacy for future generations.

In the end, both trees and wealth creation follow the same fundamental law of nature: slow, steady, and strategic growth leads to greatness.

Key take away from Chapter:

1. Strong Foundations Matter – Just like trees grow deep roots first, wealth-building starts with knowledge, discipline, and smart financial planning.

2. Growth Takes Time – Neither trees nor wealth grow overnight. Consistency and patience are key to long-term success.

3. Weather the Storms – Both trees and financial journeys face challenges. Staying strong during tough times leads to greater rewards.

4. Small Efforts Compound – A tree adds rings yearly, just as small savings and smart investments grow over time.

5. Create a Lasting Legacy – A giant tree provides shade for generations, just as wisely managed wealth benefits future family members.

Great Things Take Time

A tiny seed, so small, so light,

Grows into a tree, reaching height.

Through sun and storm, it stands so tall,

But it didn't grow in a day at all.

A river starts with drops so few,

Yet soon, its waters rush and grew.

Step by step, both slow and grand,

They shape the sky, they carve the land.

Wealth, like nature, needs its space,

Patience builds a lasting place.

Slow and steady, let it flow,

Great things take their time to grow.

CHAPTER 3

A Year of 12 Months and Four Seasons: Lessons for Life, Investment, and Wealth Management

Life, like a year, moves through different phases, each with its own opportunities and challenges. The 12 months and four seasons symbolize cycles of growth, change, and renewal. These cycles offer valuable insights into personal development, financial planning, and wealth management. Just as nature follows a rhythm, so do our financial and personal lives. Recognizing these patterns can help individuals make wise choices, manage risks, and maximize opportunities.

Spring: The Season of Beginnings and Growth

Spring represents new beginnings, fresh opportunities, and the planting of seeds. It is a time of renewal, much like the early stages of life and investment.

Life Perspective

Spring in life corresponds to childhood and youth. It is a period of learning, growth, and exploration. This is when one acquires knowledge, builds relationships, and sets the foundation for the future. Just as plants need care to grow, individuals must invest in education, skill development, and healthy habits.

Investment Insights

In investment terms, spring symbolizes the startup phase. Entrepreneurs and investors plant seeds by starting new businesses, entering the stock market, or diversifying their portfolios. This is the time for taking calculated risks and exploring opportunities for growth. The focus should be on research, learning market trends, and making informed decisions.

Wealth Management Strategies

Spring is the right time to start saving and investing. Developing a disciplined saving habit, setting long-term financial goals, and building an emergency fund can provide financial security. This is also the best time to invest in stocks, real estate, or mutual funds with long-term growth potential.

Summer: The Season of Hard Work and Expansion

Summer is a period of action, prosperity, and endurance. The seeds planted in spring grow strong, but they require nurturing and protection from external challenges.

Life Perspective

In life, summer represents young adulthood and mid-career growth. This is a phase of hard work, professional expansion, and wealth accumulation. Individuals take on responsibilities, establish families, and focus on career development. Consistency and perseverance are key to success during this period.

Investment Insights

For investors, summer signifies the growth phase. Markets expand, businesses flourish, and profits start to materialize. However, just like summer heat can sometimes be extreme, financial markets can become volatile. Investors must be prepared to weather fluctuations and make adjustments when necessary. Diversification and risk management are essential to sustaining financial growth.

Wealth Management Strategies

During this stage, individuals should focus on wealth accumulation, optimizing their investments, and increasing income sources. This is the right time to strengthen retirement plans, invest in real estate, and build passive income streams. Staying updated on market trends and revisiting investment portfolios ensures stability and continuous growth.

Autumn: The Season of Reaping Rewards and Adjustments

Autumn is a time of harvest, reflection, and preparation. It represents the transition from active growth to careful planning for the future.

Life Perspective

In life, autumn corresponds to middle age, when individuals enjoy the fruits of their hard work. It is a time of career stability, family responsibilities, and financial security. However, just as leaves fall, changes are inevitable—children grow up, career paths shift, and new responsibilities arise.

Investment Insights

For investors, autumn is the period of reaping rewards. Investments made earlier should now yield substantial returns. However, this is also a time for reassessment. Some investments may need to be reallocated or withdrawn to ensure long-term stability. A strategic approach to financial planning is crucial to prepare for the next phase.

Wealth Management Strategies

This stage requires a balance between maintaining wealth and preparing for retirement. Debt reduction, tax planning, and estate management become key priorities. Creating passive income sources, such as dividends or rental income, ensures financial independence. Reviewing insurance policies and updating wills help secure a stable future for oneself and loved ones.

Winter: The Season of Preservation and Legacy

Winter symbolizes rest, preservation, and reflection. It is a time to slow down, appreciate achievements, and ensure stability for the next generation.

Life Perspective

In life, winter represents old age and retirement. It is a phase of wisdom, reflection, and passing on knowledge to future generations. Maintaining health, enjoying personal passions, and nurturing family bonds become priorities.

Investment Insights

Winter in investments signifies a period of capital preservation. Risk-taking decreases, and the focus shifts to maintaining financial security. Conservative investments, such as bonds, fixed deposits, and annuities, become essential. The goal is to enjoy financial independence without unnecessary exposure to market risks.

Wealth Management Strategies

In this phase, estate planning, wealth transfer, and charitable contributions become important. Individuals should ensure that their financial legacy benefits their family and society. A well-structured retirement plan allows one to live comfortably without financial stress. This is also the time to mentor younger generations in financial literacy and decision-making.

Conclusion

A year with 12 months and four seasons mirrors the journey of life, investment, and wealth management. Recognizing the patterns of growth, preservation, and transition helps individuals make better financial and personal decisions. Just as farmers respect the changing seasons, investors and individuals must understand economic cycles, personal financial needs, and long-term goals.

By aligning life and financial strategies with the wisdom of the seasons, one can achieve stability, success, and a lasting legacy. Whether planting new seeds in spring, working hard in summer, reaping rewards in autumn, or preserving wealth in winter, each phase offers valuable lessons. The key to a prosperous life lies in understanding these cycles and making thoughtful, well-planned decisions at every stage.

Key take away from Chapter:

1. **Recognizing Life and Financial Cycles Helps in Better Planning**

   Just as nature moves through different seasons, life and investments follow a cycle of growth, expansion, reaping rewards, and preservation. Understanding these patterns allows individuals to make strategic decisions that align with their life stages and financial goals.

2. **Spring: The Time to Learn, Invest, and Lay Foundations**

   The early stages of life and investment resemble spring, where new opportunities arise, and foundational work is crucial. Education, skill-building, and disciplined saving are essential, much like planting seeds for future financial security.

3. **Summer: A Period of Hard Work and Wealth Accumulation**

   Summer represents career growth and financial expansion. This is the time for maximizing earnings, managing risks, and ensuring long-term investments are nurtured. Just as summer heat requires resilience, financial markets may experience volatility, requiring careful risk management.

4. **Autumn: Reaping Rewards and Making Strategic Adjustments**

Middle age and the mature investment phase symbolize autumn—a time to enjoy the fruits of past efforts while preparing for future stability. Smart financial decisions, wealth reallocation, and retirement planning ensure that success is sustained beyond active working years.

5. **Winter: The Focus on Preservation, Legacy, and Stability**

Retirement and the later years mirror winter, where financial security and legacy planning take priority. Minimizing risks, ensuring passive income, estate planning, and mentoring the next generation help secure a comfortable and meaningful life beyond active work.

By aligning financial decisions with life's natural cycles, individuals can create a well-structured wealth management strategy that ensures long-term prosperity and stability.

The Rhythm of Time

January starts with frosty light,

February warms with love so bright.

March and April bring the bloom,

May and June, the sun in tune.

July's wealth in golden fields,

August reaps what hard work yields.

September calls with falling leaves,

October glows as autumn weaves.

November slows in calm embrace,

December ends with joy and grace.

Through months and seasons, life unfolds,

With wealth in love and dreams we hold.

CHAPTER 4

Mount Everest is Climb by Humans; and The Big Wealth is

Mount Everest, standing at 8,848 meters above sea level, is Earth's highest peak and a symbol of human aspiration and resilience. Since the historic ascent by Sir Edmund Hillary and Tenzing Norgay in 1953, thousands have attempted to reach its summit, each facing formidable challenges. The journey to the top of Everest parallels the path of wealth creation, where vision, determination, and strategic planning are essential.

Challenges of Climbing Mount Everest

Climbing Everest presents numerous obstacles:

Extreme Altitude: Above 8,000 meters, known as the "death zone," the air contains only a third of the oxygen at sea level, leading to severe altitude sickness.

Unpredictable Weather: Sudden storms can introduce life-threatening conditions, making timing and adaptability crucial.

Treacherous Terrain: Climbers navigate icefalls, crevasses, and steep ascents, requiring meticulous planning and physical endurance.

These challenges necessitate not only physical preparation but also mental fortitude and strategic decision-making.

Parallels Between Summiting Everest and Wealth Creation

The endeavor to summit Everest mirrors the journey of building substantial wealth:

Vision and Goal Setting: Both climbers and entrepreneurs begin with a clear, ambitious objective.

Resilience and Perseverance: Overcoming setbacks, whether in mountaineering or business, is essential for success.

Calculated Risk-Taking: Assessing and managing risks can prevent catastrophic failures.

Continuous Learning and Adaptation: Adapting to changing conditions and learning from experiences are vital.

Profiles of the World's Wealthiest Individuals

As of February 2025, the top five wealthiest individuals are from source forbes:

Elon Musk: With a net worth of $433.9 billion, Musk's ventures include Tesla, SpaceX, and xAI.

His relentless innovation and industry disruption have been key to his success.

Jeff Bezos: Founder of Amazon, Bezos has amassed $233.5 billion. His focus on customer experience and diversification has propelled Amazon to global dominance.

Larry Ellison: With $209.7 billion, Ellison's Oracle Corporation revolutionized database management systems, showcasing the importance of technological advancement.

Mark Zuckerberg: Co-founder of Meta Platforms, Zuckerberg's $202.5 billion fortune stems from his vision of a connected world, emphasizing the power of social networks.

Bernard Arnault & Family: Leading LVMH, Arnault's $168.8 billion wealth highlights the value of luxury brands and strategic acquisitions.

Wealth Creation Lessons from Their Journeys

Embrace Innovation: Musk's ventures demonstrate that pushing technological boundaries can lead to unprecedented success.

Customer-Centric Approach: Bezos's emphasis on customer satisfaction has been a cornerstone of Amazon's growth.

Strategic Risk Management: Ellison's calculated risks in software development underscore the importance of informed decision-making.

Visionary Thinking: Zuckerberg's foresight in social media's potential transformed global communication.

Leveraging Heritage and Brand Value: Arnault's focus on luxury brands shows the enduring worth of quality and tradition.

India's Wealthiest Individuals and Their Journeys

India, with its rapidly growing economy, has produced numerous billionaires whose journeys offer valuable insights into wealth creation. As of January 2025, the top five wealthiest Indians are from source forbes:

Mukesh Ambani: Chairman of Reliance Industries, Ambani's net worth stands at $119.5 billion. Under his leadership, Reliance expanded from petrochemicals to telecommunications and retail, emphasizing diversification and innovation.

Gautam Adani: Founder of the Adani Group, Adani has a net worth of $116 billion. Starting as a commodities trader, he ventured into infrastructure, energy, and logistics, highlighting the importance of strategic expansion.

Savitri Jindal & Family: With a net worth of $43.7 billion, the Jindal family's wealth comes from the O.P. Jindal Group, a leader in steel production. Their success underscores the value of industrial prowess and succession planning.

Shiv Nadar: Founder of HCL Technologies, Nadar's net worth is $40.2 billion. His focus on information technology services and products showcases the potential of the tech industry in wealth creation.

Dilip Shanghvi: With $29.8 billion, Shanghvi founded Sun Pharmaceutical Industries, emphasizing the significance of the pharmaceutical sector and strategic acquisitions.

Wealth Creation Lessons from Indian Billionaires

Diversification and Innovation: Ambani's expansion into various sectors illustrates the benefits of diversification and embracing new technologies.

Strategic Expansion: Adani's journey from trading to infrastructure development highlights the importance of seizing growth opportunities.

Industrial Prowess: The Jindal family's focus on core industries like steel demonstrates the value of specialization and operational excellence.

Embracing Technology: Nadar's success with HCL Technologies underscores the potential of the IT sector and continuous innovation.

Strategic Acquisitions: Shanghvi's growth through acquisitions in the pharmaceutical industry highlights the importance of strategic investments.

Key take away from Chapter:

1. Vision and Strategic Planning: Success, whether in summiting Everest or wealth creation, begins with a clear goal and a well-defined strategy.

2. Resilience and Risk Management: Overcoming setbacks, managing risks, and adapting to challenges are crucial for long-term success.

3. Diversification and Innovation: Expanding into new sectors and embracing technological advancements drive sustainable growth.

4. Continuous Learning and Adaptation: Staying informed, evolving with changing conditions, and refining strategies lead to enduring success.

5. Endurance and Perseverance: Whether in business or mountaineering, sustained effort, persistence, and calculated decisions are essential to achieving greatness.

"Climbing Wealth, Inspired by Nature"

Mount Everest stands so high,

Climbers reach it, though storms may lie.

Wealth, like Everest, needs a steady climb,

Step by step, with patience and time.

Nature teaches growth, balance, and flow,

Wealth grows the same when you truly know.

Tools for climbers, knowledge for wealth,

Both need protection, like nature's stealth.

Climb your wealth mountain, learn from the earth,

For nature's wisdom holds infinite worth.

CHAPTER 5

Choose your Plant Wisely in Garden and Sources of Wealth

Gardening and wealth creation share striking similarities. Both require patience, planning, and the right selection of elements to yield fruitful results. Choosing the right plants for your garden is as crucial as selecting the right avenues for wealth generation. A well-maintained garden enhances the environment, improves mental health, and provides food, shade, and beauty. Similarly, sound financial decisions lead to prosperity, while poor choices can cause financial ruin.

This note explores the importance of selecting the right plants for a garden—highlighting both positive and negative aspects of certain trees, fruits, and flowers—before drawing parallels with various wealth creation and destruction avenues.

1. Choosing the Right Plants for Your Garden

The trees and plants you choose for your garden should align with your goals. Some trees bear nutritious fruits, others provide fragrant flowers, while some can become a nuisance over time.

Let's explore both the positive and negative aspects of different plants.

A. Positive Choices for a Garden

Mango Tree (Mangifera indica)

Benefits: Produces delicious, nutritious fruits rich in vitamins. Provides shade, enhances oxygen levels, and adds beauty.

Consideration: Requires warm climate and space to grow properly.

Coconut Tree (Cocos nucifera)

Benefits: Multipurpose tree with edible fruit, water, and oil. Symbol of abundance and prosperity.

Consideration: Needs ample water and tropical conditions.

Neem Tree (Azadirachta indica)

Benefits: Medicinal properties, natural pesticide, air purifier.

Consideration: Bitter fruit, not ideal for edible use, but valuable for environmental health.

Lemon Tree (Citrus limon)

Benefits: Produces vitamin-rich fruits, used in culinary and medicinal applications. Compact and easy to grow.

Consideration: Requires sunlight and protection from pests.

Rose Plant (Rosa spp.)

Benefits: Beautiful flowers with fragrance, symbolizing love and positivity. Used in cosmetics and perfumes.

Consideration: Thorns can cause injury, and plants require maintenance.

Bamboo (Bambusoideae family)

Benefits: Fast-growing, provides oxygen, used in construction and decoration. Brings prosperity in some cultures.

Consideration: Can spread aggressively if not managed.

B. **Negative Choices for a Garden**

Eucalyptus Tree (Eucalyptus spp.)

Downside: Absorbs a large amount of water, making it unsuitable for dry regions. May deplete soil nutrients.

Cotton Tree (Bombax ceiba)

Downside: Sheds excessive fibers, creating maintenance issues. Not ideal for urban areas.

Pine Trees (Pinus spp.)

Downside: Acidic needles can affect soil quality, and fallen pine cones require regular cleaning.

Datura (Datura stramonium)

Downside: Poisonous plant, though it has medicinal uses, it can be harmful if ingested accidentally.

Conclusion on Gardening Choices

A well-planned garden enhances beauty, provides fresh air, and contributes to sustainability. Similarly, poor choices can create problems, requiring more effort to maintain than they are worth.

2. Sources of Wealth Creation and Destruction

Like gardening, wealth-building depends on careful planning and wise choices. Some avenues create long-term prosperity, while others lead to financial trouble.

A. Positive Wealth Creation Avenues

Investing in Stocks

Benefits: Potential for high returns over time.

Consideration: Requires knowledge and patience to navigate market fluctuations.

Real Estate Investment

Benefits: Appreciation in property value, rental income, and asset security.

Consideration: Requires initial capital, market research, and proper maintenance.

Entrepreneurship and Business

Benefits: High potential for wealth, job creation, and economic impact.

Consideration: Requires risk-taking, innovation, and continuous effort.

Mutual Funds and ETFs

Benefits: Diversified investment with professional management.

Consideration: Market risks and fund management fees.

Gold and Precious Metals

Benefits: Hedge against inflation and economic instability.

Consideration: Value fluctuations and storage concerns.

Intellectual Property and Digital Assets

Benefits: Passive income through books, music, patents, and online businesses.

Consideration: Requires creativity, copyright protection, and market demand.

Education and Skill Development

Benefits: Higher earning potential and career growth.

Consideration: Requires time, effort, and financial investment.

B. Negative Wealth Destruction Avenues

Gambling and Speculation

Downside: High risk of loss with little control over outcomes.

Unplanned Debt and Loans

Downside: Leads to financial burden if not managed properly.

Ponzi Schemes and Fraudulent Investments

Downside: Loss of capital due to scams and fraudulent schemes.

Overconsumption and Lifestyle Inflation

Downside: Spending beyond means leads to financial stress.

Lack of Financial Planning

Downside: Poor savings and investment habits cause instability.

Conclusion on Wealth Choices

Just as choosing the wrong plant can ruin a garden, poor financial decisions can destroy wealth. Strategic planning, education, and disciplined investments help create a stable financial future.

Final Thoughts

Both gardening and wealth-building require foresight and patience. A well-chosen plant enhances a garden, just as a well-planned investment ensures financial security. Understanding the positives and negatives of each choice leads to long-term benefits in both fields.

Key take away from Chapter:

1. Choose Plants Wisely for a Healthy Garden – Selecting trees and plants with long-term benefits, such as fruit-bearing or medicinal plants, enhances the beauty and sustainability of a garden. Avoid plants with invasive roots or excessive maintenance needs.

2. Good Investments Yield Long-Term Rewards – Wealth creation requires strategic investments in stocks, real estate, mutual funds and businesses, just as a well-planned garden thrives with the right plants.

3. Avoid Wealth-Draining Choices – Just as some trees harm soil and resources, financial mistakes like excessive debt, gambling, and scams can erode wealth over time.

4. Diversification Ensures Stability – A balanced mix of different plants in a garden supports ecological health, just as diversifying investments

minimizes financial risks and promotes steady growth.

5. Patience and Planning Lead to Growth – Whether cultivating a garden or building wealth, success comes with careful planning, continuous learning, and long-term commitment.

"Plant Wisely, Grow Wealth Strongly"

A garden blooms with plants you choose,

Pick the wrong ones, and you may lose.

Some grow fast, but fade away,

Others stay strong, come what may.

Wealth is the same — choose your source,

Quick gains may fail, but steady stays the course.

Plant strong seeds like hard work and skill,

Water with patience, and wealth will fill.

A wise gardener builds a garden grand,

Like wealth that grows with a steady hand.

CHAPTER 6

Earth is Round – History Repeats Again & Again

Lessons on Life, Markets, and Wealth Creation

History is filled with patterns that repeat themselves. Just as sailors once proved that the Earth is round by observing ships disappearing over the horizon, history, markets, and wealth creation follow cycles that demonstrate the same recurring truths. What has happened before will likely happen again, albeit in different forms. The key is recognizing these patterns and learning from them to make better decisions in life and business.

This lesson explores how history repeats itself in various aspects of life, the financial markets, and wealth creation. We will analyze both the positive and negative aspects of these cycles and how we can apply these lessons to navigate the future more effectively.

The Cycles of History and Life

Throughout history, civilizations have risen and fallen in cycles. Societies have experienced periods of innovation, growth, decline, and rebirth. The same applies to human lives—we experience ups and downs, progress and setbacks, triumphs and failures.

Examples from History:

The Fall of Rome and Modern Parallels

Rome's decline was due to economic instability, overexpansion, corruption, and external threats.

Similar patterns can be seen in the fall of great empires like the British Empire and challenges facing modern superpowers.

The Renaissance and Rebirth of Knowledge

After the Dark Ages, Europe rediscovered ancient wisdom, leading to massive advancements in art, science, and trade.

Today, we see similar renaissances in technology and innovation, such as the AI revolution.

Lesson for Life:

Periods of difficulty are often followed by growth and opportunity.

Understanding historical patterns helps us anticipate challenges and prepare better.

Market Cycles – Boom, Bust, and Recovery

Financial markets are not random; they follow predictable cycles of boom, bust, and recovery.

Understanding these cycles is key to making informed investment decisions.

Historical Market Cycles:

The Great Depression (1929–1939) and the 2008 Financial Crisis

Both were triggered by excessive risk-taking, speculation, and weak regulation.

After each crash, economies eventually recovered, often emerging stronger.

The Dot-Com Bubble (1990s) and Cryptocurrency Crashes

The internet boom led to excessive valuations, followed by a market crash.

Cryptocurrencies have followed a similar pattern, with extreme highs and lows.

Lessons for Investors:

Every boom is followed by a bust; overconfidence can be dangerous.

Those who stay prepared and invest wisely during downturns often emerge wealthier.

Understanding cycles allows investors to buy low and sell high.

The Wealth Creation Cycle – From Rags to Riches to Rags

Wealth creation is also cyclical. Many families and businesses go from poverty to prosperity, only to lose their wealth over generations.

Examples of Wealth Cycles:

The Vanderbilt Family

Cornelius Vanderbilt built immense wealth in shipping and railroads.

By the third generation, much of the family fortune had been squandered.

Silicon Valley's Self-Made Billionaires

Tech entrepreneurs like Elon Musk and Jeff Bezos started with little and built empires.

Some tech fortunes are already facing challenges due to market cycles and economic shifts.

Points to focus for Wealth Creation:

Building wealth requires vision, discipline, and hard work.

Preserving wealth requires careful planning, education, and long-term thinking.

Many fortunes are lost due to lack of discipline, entitlement, or mismanagement.

The Positive Side of History Repeating Itself

While repeating history may sound negative, it also means that opportunities arise again and again.

Positive Cycles:

Innovation and Economic Growth

Despite recessions, human innovation always drives new industries.

The invention of the steam engine, the internet, and artificial intelligence have all created new economic booms.

The Power of Second Chances

History teaches us that failure is not final.

Many successful entrepreneurs failed before achieving greatness (e.g., Steve Jobs, Thomas Edison).

How to Benefit from These Cycles:

Stay informed and adaptable.

Recognize downturns as opportunities rather than disasters.

Learn from past mistakes and continuously improve.

The Negative Side of History Repeating Itself

Unfortunately, negative cycles also repeat when people fail to learn from history.

Negative Cycles:

Economic Crashes Due to Greed and Speculation

Every financial crisis has been fueled by greed, speculation, and ignoring risk.

Wars and Political Instability

The world has repeatedly seen conflicts arise from nationalism, economic struggles, and political power plays.

Ignoring Warnings and Making the Same Mistakes

Many companies fail because they refuse to adapt (e.g., Blockbuster, Kodak).

How to Avoid Negative Cycles:

Study history to avoid past mistakes.

Stay disciplined in investing and business.

Focus on long-term thinking rather than short-term gains.

Conclusion: Learning from History to Shape a Better Future

The Earth is round, and history moves in cycles, bringing both challenges and opportunities. Understanding these repeating patterns in life, markets, and wealth creation allows us to make better decisions and avoid common pitfalls.

Final Lessons:

Accept that ups and downs are natural and prepare accordingly.

Use history as a guide for making smarter life and financial decisions.

Recognize opportunities in downturns and avoid excessive greed during booms.

By applying these lessons, we can navigate life and business more effectively, ensuring long-term success rather than being caught in destructive cycles.

Key take away from Chapter:

1. History Moves in Cycles – Life, markets, and wealth follow repeating patterns of rise, fall, and recovery. Recognizing these cycles helps us make better decisions.

2. Booms Are Always Followed by Busts – Financial markets and economies experience highs and lows. Smart investors prepare for downturns and capitalize on recoveries.

3. Wealth Creation Requires Discipline – Building wealth is hard, but keeping it is even harder. Many fortunes are lost due to mismanagement and lack of long-term vision.

4. Opportunities Always Return – Every crisis brings new opportunities. Innovation and human resilience create new industries and wealth, even after setbacks.

5. Learn from History to Avoid Mistakes – Many failures occur because people ignore past lessons. Studying history helps us avoid repeated mistakes in life, business, and investing.

"The Earth Turns, Wealth Returns"

The earth is round, it spins each day,

Just like wealth that comes and sways.

Rains may flood, then dry lands appear,

Wealth too rises, then may disappear.

Tulip Mania once made fortunes fly,

Like stock bubbles that touch the sky.

Seasons repeat, so does wealth's fate,

Booms and busts come, early or late.

Learn from nature, stay steady and sound,

For wealth, like earth, always comes around.

CHAPTER 7

Respect Professionals & Mentors – They May Have Third Eye to See Things Differently

Introduction

Mentors and professionals bring years of experience and wisdom that allow them to see things from a different perspective, much like having a "third eye" — a vision beyond the ordinary. Their advice can help navigate challenges, avoid mistakes, and seize opportunities that may not be immediately visible. Throughout history, from ancient epics like the Mahabharata and Ramayana to modern sports and wealth management, those who respected their mentors often achieved greatness, while those who ignored wise counsel faced downfall.

The Role of Mentors in Mahabharata

1. Dronacharya and Arjuna – The Power of Dedication to a Mentor

Dronacharya, the master of warfare, saw extraordinary potential in Arjuna and guided him to become the greatest archer of his time. Despite having other students, Drona's special attention to Arjuna was because of his dedication and respect for his guru.

Situation:

During a training session, Drona placed a wooden bird on a tree and asked each student to aim at its eye. Before allowing them to shoot, he asked what they saw. Most described the tree, the bird, or the surrounding environment. Only Arjuna said, "I see only the eye of the bird." This clarity of vision was due to his training and trust in his guru's methods.

Lesson for Wealth Creation & Management:

In financial planning, success comes to those who focus and listen to the guidance of experienced professionals. Just as Arjuna didn't get distracted, an investor who follows a well-planned strategy by financial mentors can achieve wealth without being misled by market noise.

2. **Krishna's Guidance to Arjuna – The Bhagavad Gita as the Ultimate Mentorship**

During the Kurukshetra war, Arjuna was confused and emotionally broken. At this crucial moment, Krishna, his mentor, revealed the Bhagavad Gita, providing wisdom on duty, righteousness, and vision beyond immediate challenges.

Situation:

Arjuna was hesitant to fight against his own family members. Krishna, acting as his divine mentor, explained that duty and righteousness (Dharma) must guide decisions rather than emotions. This advice helped Arjuna regain his focus and fight the battle with clarity.

Lesson for Business & Investments:

A successful entrepreneur or investor may face moments of doubt, like during a market crash or business crisis. A good mentor provides clarity, helping one make logical, long-term decisions rather than acting emotionally.

3. Vidura's Advice to Dhritarashtra – Ignored Wisdom Leads to Disaster

Vidura, the wise minister of Hastinapura, consistently warned King Dhritarashtra about the dangers of Duryodhana's greed and arrogance. However, the king ignored these warnings, leading to the destruction of his dynasty.

Situation:

Vidura advised Dhritarashtra to prevent the war by restraining Duryodhana and treating the Pandavas fairly. But Dhritarashtra, blinded by attachment to his son, ignored Vidura's counsel. The result was the complete destruction of the Kaurava clan.

Lesson for Wealth Management:

Many investors ignore the advice of financial experts, getting tempted by high-risk investments or emotional decisions. Just like Dhritarashtra's blindness led to ruin, ignoring sound financial advice can result in heavy losses.

The Role of Mentors in Ramayana

1. Vashishta's Guidance to Rama – Strength in Wisdom

Sage Vashishta, the royal guru of Ayodhya, mentored young Rama, providing him with wisdom, discipline, and a strong foundation for leadership.

Situation:

Before embarking on his journey of exile, Rama had to face various hardships, but his mentor's teachings kept him calm and composed. Even when faced with betrayal and injustice, Rama upheld righteousness (Dharma), following the lessons of his guru.

Lesson for Leaders & Entrepreneurs:

A strong foundation built under a great mentor helps leaders stay resilient during tough times.

Business leaders who seek mentorship before taking on big ventures often handle challenges better than those who go in unprepared.

2. Hanuman's Counsel to Sugriva – The Right Guidance Brings Success

Sugriva, the vanara king, had lost his kingdom to his brother Vali and was living in fear. Hanuman, a wise strategist and devotee of Rama, advised Sugriva to form an alliance with Rama, which led to his victory.

Situation:

Sugriva doubted Rama's ability to defeat Vali. However, Hanuman assured him of Rama's power. Taking this advice, Sugriva sought Rama's help, eventually regaining his kingdom.

Lesson for Businesses & Investments:

Seeking guidance from financial or business mentors can open opportunities that might not be visible otherwise. Like Sugriva, trusting the right advisor can lead to success.

The Role of Coaches in Successful Sports Careers

1. Ramakant Achrekar – The Coach Behind Sachin Tendulkar

Sachin Tendulkar, one of the greatest cricketers of all time, credited his success to his coach, Ramakant Achrekar.

Situation:

Achrekar made young Sachin practice for hours, even placing a coin on the stumps as a reward for remaining not out. This discipline and training shaped Sachin's legendary career.

Lesson for Wealth Management:

Just like disciplined training in sports, disciplined investing leads to long-term financial success. Consistently following a mentor's financial strategies helps in wealth creation.

2. **Phil Jackson – The Coach Behind Michael Jordan & Kobe Bryant**

Phil Jackson, known for his deep understanding of basketball psychology, guided players like Michael Jordan and Kobe Bryant to become legends.

Situation:

Jackson introduced mindfulness and team-focused strategies, helping Jordan and Bryant control their egos and focus on teamwork, leading to multiple championships.

Lesson for Entrepreneurs & Investors:

A good mentor teaches patience and strategic thinking, both crucial for sustained success in business and investments.

How Respecting Mentors Translates to Wealth Creation

Long-Term Vision:

Warren Buffett had Benjamin Graham as his mentor, who taught him value investing principles. Following these, Buffett became one of the richest investors.

Discipline and Learning:

Like athletes training under great coaches, investors who listen to financial advisors and follow systematic investment strategies grow their wealth steadily.

Avoiding Pitfalls:

Many investors lose money due to greed or panic. Just like Krishna guided Arjuna, a good financial mentor helps investors stay calm during market crashes.

Networking and Growth:

Being around the right professionals opens up wealth-building opportunities, just as Sugriva's alliance with Rama led to success.

Conclusion

The greatest minds in history, whether in war, business, or sports, have had mentors who shaped their success.

Ignoring the advice of experienced professionals often leads to failure, while respecting them leads to growth and stability.

The "third eye" of a mentor is their ability to see beyond the present, guiding their mentees toward success.

Whether in financial management, business strategy, or personal development, listening to those who have already walked the path can help avoid mistakes and achieve greatness.

Key take away from Chapter:

1. **Mentors Provide Clarity & Vision Beyond the Present**

   Just like Krishna guided Arjuna in the Bhagavad Gita, great mentors help their mentees make rational, long-term decisions rather than reacting emotionally to challenges.

2. **Respecting Professional Advice Prevents Costly Mistakes**

   Ignoring wise counsel, like Dhritarashtra ignored Vidura's warnings, often leads to downfall—whether in war, business, or personal finance. Seeking expert advice can help avoid major losses.

3. **Discipline & Consistency Lead to Greatness**

Just as Sachin Tendulkar's success came from disciplined training under coach Ramakant Achrekar, financial success requires consistent investing and patience under expert guidance.

4. **Right Mentorship Opens Doors to Opportunities**

Sugriva regained his lost kingdom by trusting Hanuman's counsel and forming an alliance with Rama. Similarly, in business and wealth creation, the right mentor can introduce opportunities that might otherwise go unnoticed.

5. **Strategic Thinking & Long-Term Vision Are Crucial for Success**

Successful investors like Warren Buffett followed their mentors' investment philosophies to build lasting wealth. Whether in business, sports, or finance, those who respect and follow strategic advice achieve sustained success.

"The Third Eye Sees Wealth Beyond"

A tree grows tall, but roots stay deep,

Like mentors' wisdom, in silence they keep.

They see market storms before they appear,

Like nature sensing rain when skies aren't clear.

Wealth creation, like seeds, needs right care,

Mentors guide you when risks are unfair.

They know when to sow, and when to reap,

Helping your wealth grow, wide and deep.

Respect their vision, for they clearly see,

What you may miss — your wealth's true destiny.

CHAPTER 8

River Stays Full with Multiple Waterfalls: A Wealth Accumulation Analogy

Introduction

Nature provides profound lessons on sustainability, growth, and abundance. One such lesson is found in the way rivers remain full—by receiving water from multiple waterfalls, streams, and tributaries. A river that depends on just one source is vulnerable to drought, but one that receives water from many sources stays vibrant and full throughout the year. This natural phenomenon mirrors financial stability, where wealth accumulation is best achieved through multiple income streams rather than relying on a single source.

In this note, we will explore the concept of financial abundance by drawing parallels between rivers and multiple sources of income. We will also examine key wealth accumulation strategies inspired by this analogy, providing insights into how one can ensure financial security and growth.

1. **The River and Wealth: A Powerful Analogy**

A river symbolizes financial stability, while waterfalls and tributaries represent income streams. Just as a river's flow is strengthened by numerous water sources, financial security is enhanced when multiple income streams feed into one's wealth.

Dependence on One Source is Risky: A river that depends on a single source may run dry in times of drought, just as a person relying on only one income source is vulnerable to job loss, business failure, or economic downturns.

Diversification Ensures Stability: A river with multiple sources remains full even if one dries up. Similarly, having multiple income streams protects against financial uncertainties.

Expansion and Growth: Rivers expand and nourish lands due to their abundant flow, just as diversified wealth enables investment, security, and growth opportunities.

2. **The Importance of Multiple Income Streams**

The modern financial landscape is unpredictable. Relying solely on a job or one business can be risky. Creating multiple streams of income is essential for long-term wealth.

Types of Income Streams

Earned Income: Salary or wages from employment.

Business Income: Profits from entrepreneurial ventures.

Investment Income: Dividends, stock or mutual funds appreciation, and real estate appreciation.

Passive Income: Earnings from assets like rental properties, royalties, or online businesses.

Residual Income: Earnings that continue after the work is completed (e.g., book royalties, online courses).

Interest Income: Returns from fixed deposits, bonds, and lending capital.

Just as a river gets replenished from different waterfalls, one must aim to have multiple income sources to ensure consistent wealth flow.

3. **The Strategy of Small Streams Leading to a Big River**

Even small waterfalls contribute to a mighty river. In wealth accumulation, small but steady income streams, when combined, create substantial financial security.

Steps to Implement This Strategy

Start Small but Consistently: Begin with small investment opportunities like mutual funds, side hustles, or digital businesses.

Diversify Gradually: Expand income streams by reinvesting profits from one source into another.

Automate Growth: Use passive income strategies like rental properties, automated online businesses, or stock/mutual fund investments that compound over time.

Over time, these small streams will collectively form a large, strong river of wealth.

4. **Building Passive Income Like a Continuous Waterfall**

A waterfall flows continuously without external effort. Similarly, passive income should be designed to generate money with minimal ongoing effort.

Key Passive Income Strategies

Real Estate Investments: Rental properties provide a steady cash flow.

Stock Market Investments: Dividend-paying stocks create residual income.

Online Businesses: Digital assets like e-books, courses, and affiliate marketing generate passive earnings.

Intellectual Property: Royalties from patents, books, or music continue long after the initial effort.

The goal is to create multiple such "waterfalls" to keep financial flow uninterrupted.

5. Reinvestment: The River's Self-Sustaining Cycle

A river does not just receive water—it also reinvests by nourishing lands and feeding other water bodies. Similarly, wealth must be reinvested to ensure long-term growth.

Reinvestment Strategies

Compounding: Let investment returns generate further earnings through reinvestment.

Business Expansion: Use profits from one venture to fund another.

Education & Skill Growth: Invest in self-improvement to increase earning potential.

By continuously reinvesting, one ensures a growing and self-sustaining financial river.

6. Risk Management: Preparing for Dry Seasons

Even rivers face seasonal dry spells, but their multiple sources help them survive. Similarly, financial planning should account for risks and downturns.

Risk Management Techniques

Emergency Fund: Maintain liquid cash reserves.

Insurance: Protect assets and income sources with appropriate insurance policies.

Diversification: Spread investments across different sectors to minimize losses.

Risk management ensures that financial stability is maintained even during economic downturns.

7. Wealth Flow and Generational Prosperity

A river benefits not just itself but also the lands and communities around it. Similarly, wealth should be managed in a way that benefits future generations.

Wealth Preservation Strategies

Estate Planning: Proper wills and trusts prevent wealth erosion.

Financial Education: Teaching financial literacy ensures responsible wealth management by future generations.

Philanthropy: Supporting charitable causes ensures a lasting legacy.

Sustained wealth, like a great river, should nurture those who come after.

8. **Lessons from Wealthy Individuals and Successful Rivers**

Amazon River & Jeff Bezos: Just as the Amazon River is fed by countless tributaries, Amazon.com grew by diversifying income streams—from books to e-commerce, cloud computing, and beyond.

Ganga River & Traditional Business Families: The Ganges sustains civilizations, just as generational wealth sustains business dynasties by ensuring multiple income sources over generations.

Multiple Waterfalls & Billionaires: Billionaires like Warren Buffett and Elon Musk have diversified businesses across different sectors, ensuring financial stability.

These real-world examples reinforce the importance of multiple income sources.

9. **Action Plan: Creating Your Own Financial River**

To implement the lessons from this analogy, follow these steps:

Identify Your Waterfalls: List potential income sources you can create.

Start Small, Grow Big: Begin with manageable investments or side hustles.

Ensure Consistency: Establish automated financial systems for passive income.

Reinvest Wisely: Use earnings to create additional revenue streams.

Mitigate Risks: Have contingency plans like insurance and savings.

Teach & Share: Pass knowledge and wealth to future generations.

By following this structured approach, you can ensure a steady and growing financial river.

Conclusion

A river remains full and powerful when nourished by multiple waterfalls, just as financial security is ensured through multiple income sources. Depending on a single stream—whether a job, a business, or an investment—is risky. The key to sustainable wealth is diversification, reinvestment, and strategic risk management.

By implementing these principles, one can create a financial river that remains full, strong, and abundant—nourishing not just oneself but also future generations. Wealth accumulation, like a river, is not about finding one massive waterfall but about ensuring a steady, diverse, and sustainable flow.

Key take away from Chapter:

1. **Diversification is Key to Financial Stability**

   Just as a river stays full by receiving water from multiple sources, financial security comes from having multiple income streams—earned, business, passive, and investment income. Relying on a single source is risky.

2. **Small Streams Can Build a Powerful Financial River**

   Even small income streams, when combined, create significant wealth over time. Starting small with side hustles, investments, or digital assets can lead to long-term financial success.

3. **Passive Income Ensures Continuous Wealth Flow**

   Like a waterfall that keeps flowing, passive income sources (real estate, dividends, royalties, automated businesses) provide financial security without constant effort, enabling wealth accumulation.

4. **Reinvestment Fuels Growth and Longevity**

   A river sustains itself by nourishing its surroundings. Similarly, reinvesting earnings into new opportunities, education, or asset-building ensures continued financial expansion and security.

5. **Risk Management Protects Against Financial Droughts**

Rivers prepare for dry seasons by having multiple sources. Likewise, building an emergency fund, diversifying investments, and securing insurance protects wealth from unexpected downturns.

"Wealth Flows Like Waterfalls"

A river stays full, with streams all around,

Just like wealth grows when sources are found.

One waterfall dries, another will flow,

Like income streams that help wealth grow.

Salary, business, rent, or gain,

Multiple sources ease the strain.

Nature shows balance, wealth does too,

Diversify income, let riches flow through.

A river never stops, nor should your gain,

With many waterfalls, wealth will sustain.

CHAPTER 9

Board the Flight Going to Your Destination

Introduction: The Flight Analogy in Financial Planning

Imagine standing in a bustling airport, surrounded by passengers heading to different destinations. Some are on business trips, others on vacations, and a few on life-changing journeys. Each traveler has a specific goal, a set itinerary, and a well-planned route. They don't board just any flight; they board the one that takes them to their chosen destination.

Similarly, in financial planning, your wealth journey should be goal-oriented. You don't just invest randomly—you choose investments that align with your financial goals. This is where goal-based financial planning and need-based investing come into play. Just as a traveler selects a flight based on their destination, an investor must select financial instruments based on their needs, risk appetite, and financial aspirations.

Setting Your Financial Destination

Before booking a flight, you must decide where you want to go. Is it a beach holiday, a business conference, or a family visit? Likewise, in financial planning, your financial destination is your goal—buying a house, saving for your child's education, retirement planning, or building wealth etc.

Imaginary Example

A young professional, Raj, dreams of buying a house in 10 years. If he starts investing without a clear strategy, he may end up on the wrong financial path. Instead, he needs to define his goal (his financial destination) and plan accordingly.

Choosing the Right Flight – The Role of Goal-Based Planning

Once you know your destination, the next step is booking the right flight. You check flight options, pricing, layovers, and travel time. Similarly, goal-based financial planning involves selecting the right investment vehicles based on your timeline, risk tolerance, and financial requirements.

Imaginary Example

Raj has two options:

Take a direct flight – Investing in a mutual fund SIP with a defined target amount.

Take a flight with layovers – Investing in a mix of stocks and bonds to balance growth and security.

By choosing the right investment plan, he ensures he reaches his financial destination efficiently.

Ticket Pricing – The Budgeting Factor

Every flight ticket has a cost, and the price varies based on the class, airline, and booking time. Similarly, financial goals require budgeting. You need to assess how much you need to invest, how frequently, and for how long.

Imaginary Example

If Raj books his ticket (invests) early, the cost is lower (compounding works in his favor). If he waits too long, he may need to invest a higher amount to reach his goal.

Layovers and Diversification – Need-Based Investing

Some flights are direct, while others have layovers. A direct flight is ideal, but sometimes a layover can be beneficial—cheaper tickets or better travel experiences. In investing, need-based investing means choosing investments that match your risk profile and financial needs.

Imaginary Example

Raj, being young, can take some risks. He diversifies:

Equity Funds (high return, high risk) – Major part of his portfolio for long-term growth.

Debt Funds (stable returns, low risk) – For security and stability.

Gold/REITs (alternative assets) – To hedge against inflation.

This is like taking a layover in a safe airport before proceeding.

Unexpected Turbulence – Managing Risks in Financial Planning

No flight is completely smooth; turbulence is expected. Similarly, financial markets fluctuate. The key is risk management and staying on course.

Imaginary Example

During a market downturn, Raj panics. But instead of exiting investments, he consults his financial advisor, who reassures him that turbulence (market corrections) is normal. Over time, his investments recover and grow.

Upgrading to Business Class – Reviewing and Adjusting Investments

Sometimes, you get a chance to upgrade mid-flight. Likewise, as income grows, you can enhance your investment strategy by increasing SIP contributions, shifting to better funds, or rebalancing your portfolio.

Imaginary Example

Raj gets a promotion and increases his SIP contribution. This speeds up his journey to homeownership.

Landing Safely – Achieving Your Financial Goals

After careful planning, you finally land at your destination. In financial planning, reaching your goal means you have accumulated enough wealth to achieve your dream.

Imaginary Example

After 10 years, Raj successfully buys his dream home without financial stress, thanks to structured planning and disciplined investing.

Conclusion – The Importance of Financial Discipline

Just like a traveler follows check-in, security, and boarding rules, an investor must follow financial discipline—consistent investing, risk management, and periodic review.

Points to note

Define your financial goal (destination).

Choose the right investment strategy (flight).

Diversify and manage risks (layovers & turbulence).

Review and adjust your plan as needed (upgrades).

Stay disciplined and patient to achieve success (safe landing).

By aligning financial planning with a structured, goal-oriented approach, you ensure that you don't just travel aimlessly — you board the right flight to your financial destination.

Key take away from Chapter:

1. **Define Your Financial Destination** – Just like choosing a flight based on where you want to go, set clear financial goals such as buying a house, funding education, or planning for retirement.

2. **Choose the Right Investment Strategy** – Select investments that align with your goals and risk tolerance, similar to picking the best flight option (direct or with layovers) for your journey.

3. **Diversify and Manage Risks** – Just as layovers can optimize travel costs, diversifying investments across equity, debt, and alternative assets ensures stability and growth while managing market fluctuations.

4. **Review and Adjust Investments Regularly** – Just like upgrading to business class when feasible, periodically review your investment strategy and increase contributions or rebalance your portfolio as your financial situation improves.

5. **Stay Disciplined and Patient** – Market turbulence is normal, but long-term consistency in investing ensures you safely reach your financial destination without unnecessary detours.

"Board the Flight to Wealth"

A flight takes off to reach its place,

Like wealth grows with purpose and pace.

Choose the right flight, don't miss the call,

Invest in goals, not in things that fall.

A wrong flight may waste your precious time,

Just like wrong investments halt wealth's climb.

Stay focused, stay clear, know where you land,

Wealth needs direction, not a careless hand.

Board the flight that aligns with your dream,

And soon you'll sail on a wealth-growing stream.

CHAPTER 10

Doing Nothing Sometimes Can Keep Things Alive: A Perspective on Life, Nature, and Wealth

In today's world, where action is often equated with success, the wisdom of doing nothing is frequently overlooked. However, in various aspects of life—nature, health, and wealth management—strategic inaction can be the key to sustainability and growth. Nature thrives when left undisturbed, health flourishes with adequate rest, and wealth compounds when patience is exercised. Understanding this balance can lead to a more fulfilling and prosperous life.

1. Nature's Wisdom: Letting Things Grow Naturally

Nature operates in cycles, and often, human interference disrupts these natural processes rather than improving them. When left alone, ecosystems regenerate, forests flourish, and rivers carve their paths.

Examples from Nature:

A Forest Regenerates Itself: After a wildfire, nature restores balance by allowing plants to regrow and animals to repopulate. Over-intervention, such as excessive logging or artificial replanting, can hinder this natural process.

A River's Natural Flow: Damming a river can provide short-term benefits like hydroelectric power, but it often disrupts ecosystems. In contrast, a river left to flow naturally supports diverse marine life and sustains local communities.

A Tree's Growth: Pruning a tree too frequently can weaken it, while letting it grow at its own pace allows it to develop strong roots and resilience.

Life Lesson from Nature:

Sometimes, the best way to help something grow—whether a business, relationship, or personal skill—is to step back and allow natural progress to take place.

2. **The Power of Rest in Health and Well-Being**

Just as nature needs time to restore balance, our bodies and minds require moments of stillness to function optimally. Overworking, overtraining, or overthinking often leads to burnout rather than progress.

Examples in Health:

Muscle Recovery: Athletes know that muscles grow stronger not during workouts but during periods of rest. Excessive training without recovery leads to injuries and fatigue.

The Healing Process: A wound heals best when left undisturbed. Constantly touching or applying unnecessary treatments can slow recovery.

Mental Clarity Through Silence: Overanalyzing problems can cloud judgment, while taking a step back—through meditation or relaxation—often brings clarity and creative solutions.

Life Lesson:

Sometimes, doing nothing is the most effective way to heal, regain energy, and come back stronger. Just as the body needs sleep to function well, the mind and soul require moments of stillness.

3. **Wealth Management: The Power of Patience and Strategic Inaction**

The principles of nature and health also apply to wealth creation and management. Often, the best financial strategies involve not reacting impulsively and allowing time to work in your favor.

Lessons from Wealth Management:

The Magic of Compounding: Money grows when left invested over time. The longer an investment remains untouched, the greater the returns.

Avoiding Panic Selling: Market downturns are temporary. Investors who resist the urge to sell during a crash often see their portfolios recover and grow.

Letting Passive Income Work: Real estate, dividend stocks, and other income-generating assets perform best when left alone, requiring minimal active management.

Financial Minimalism: Spending less and saving more often leads to greater financial security than chasing high-risk opportunities.

Parallel to Nature and Life:

Justasatreegrowsstrongerwhenleftundisturbed, money grows through compounding.

Just as a river finds its path naturally, wealth follows a steady course when not disrupted by impulsive decisions.

Just as over-caring for a plant can harm it, over-managing investments can reduce long-term gains.

4. Relationships and Personal Growth: Giving Space to Flourish

In relationships and personal growth, excessive control can be counterproductive. Just as nature thrives when left alone, people grow best when given space and trust.

Lessons in Life and Relationships:

Over-Nurturing Can Harm: Just as overwatering a plant can kill it, micromanaging relationships can create unnecessary pressure. Trusting others and allowing them to grow independently strengthens bonds.

Allowing Growth to Happen Naturally: Personal skills and wisdom develop over time. Constantly forcing change can lead to frustration, while patience allows for organic growth.

Parenting and Leadership: The best leaders and parents guide rather than control. Giving children and employees the freedom to make mistakes and learn fosters independence and resilience.

Parallel to Nature and Wealth:

Just as a forest regenerates on its own, relationships strengthen when given space.

Just as wealth compounds with time, trust and personal growth deepen with patience.

Just as excessive pruning weakens a tree, excessive interference weakens relationships.

5. The Balance Between Action and Inaction

While strategic inaction is powerful, it doesn't mean neglecting responsibilities. The key is knowing when to act and when to step back.

Guiding Principles:

Act when intervention is necessary, but avoid excessive control.

Trust long-term processes, whether in nature, health, or finance.

Recognize that sometimes, doing nothing is the most effective action.

Conclusion: The Art of Letting Life Flow

Nature, health, and wealth all share a common lesson: growth often happens best when left undisturbed.

In nature, forests, rivers, and ecosystems flourish without constant interference.

In health, rest and recovery are just as important as action.

In wealth, patience and long-term thinking lead to greater financial success.

The art of doing nothing is not about laziness — it's about trusting the natural process of life. By understanding when to act and when to step back, we allow things to thrive in their own time, ensuring sustainable growth in all aspects of life.

Key take away from Chapter:

1. **Nature Thrives Without Excessive Intervention** – Forests, rivers, and ecosystems regenerate best when left undisturbed. Over-managing nature often disrupts its balance rather than improving it.

2. **Health and Growth Require Rest** – The body heals, muscles strengthen, and the mind gains clarity during periods of rest. Overworking or over-controlling can lead to burnout and slow progress.

3. **Wealth Compounds When Left Undisturbed** – Long-term investments grow through compounding, and panic-driven decisions often lead to financial loss. Patience and strategic inaction yield the best financial results.

4. **Relationships and Personal Growth Need Space** – Over-controlling loved ones, employees, or personal development can backfire. Trusting

the process and allowing organic growth leads to stronger bonds and better outcomes.

5. **The Right Balance Between Action and Inaction is Key** – Doing nothing doesn't mean neglecting responsibilities; it means knowing when to step back and let natural processes—whether in nature, health, or wealth—work in your favor.

"Let It Be, Let It Grow"

A tree stands still, yet grows so tall,

It does nothing, but nature does it all.

A river flows without force or fight,

Yet reaches the ocean, pure and right.

Wealth too grows when given its space,

Patience and time win the wealth race.

Over-managing may ruin the gain,

Like overwatering brings a plant to pain.

Sometimes doing nothing is the wisest way,

Let wealth breathe — it will grow each day.

CHAPTER 11

Airbags Open Rarely, but They May Save Lives

Understanding the Concept

Airbags in a car are designed to deploy only in extreme situations—when a severe impact occurs. Most of the time, they remain unnoticed, hidden within the dashboard or steering wheel. However, when an accident happens, they inflate within milliseconds, protecting passengers from serious injuries. This rare but crucial activation can mean the difference between life and death.

Similarly, financial protection in the form of insurance works in the same way. Policies like life, health, accident, house, and vehicle insurance remain unused for years. People often see them as unnecessary expenses, questioning their need. However, when a financial emergency strikes—a sudden death, a medical crisis, an accident, or property damage—these insurance policies act as financial airbags, absorbing the impact and preventing catastrophic losses.

Why Do People Ignore Financial Airbags?

Many individuals hesitate to invest in insurance due to common misconceptions:

"It won't happen to me." – People assume they won't face accidents, illnesses, or financial crises.

"It's an unnecessary cost." – Until they face an emergency, insurance premiums seem like an avoidable expense.

"I can manage with savings." – While savings are crucial, they might not be enough for unexpected large expenses.

"I'll buy it later." – Procrastination often leads to being unprepared when disaster strikes.

Just as cars come with airbags despite drivers hoping never to use them, individuals must have financial protection in place—even if they never need to claim it.

The Role of Financial Airbags in Different Aspects of Life

1. Life Insurance – A Lifeline for Dependents

Just as airbags cushion a crash impact, life insurance cushions the financial impact of losing a breadwinner.

The rare event of premature death can leave families in financial distress, making a life insurance payout crucial.

2. Health Insurance – Shielding Against Medical Emergencies

Medical emergencies don't happen daily, but when they do, they can drain savings.

Health insurance ensures that treatment is accessible without financial worries.

3. Accident Insurance – Support in Times of Crisis

Most people never meet with severe accidents, but those who do face heavy medical bills and loss of income.

Accident insurance provides financial support, helping individuals and families recover without additional stress.

4. Home Insurance – Safeguarding a Major Asset

Natural disasters or thefts are rare but can be financially devastating.

House insurance ensures that damages don't lead to massive monetary losses.

5. Vehicle Insurance – Protection on the Road

Just as airbags prevent serious injuries in accidents, vehicle insurance prevents financial losses due to damages, liabilities, or theft.

Final Thoughts

Airbags don't prevent accidents but significantly reduce the damage caused when an accident occurs. Likewise, insurance doesn't stop unfortunate events from happening but ensures they don't turn into financial disasters. While many people may never need to use their insurance policies, having them in place is crucial—because when an emergency does strike, it can be life-saving.

Message: It's better to have a financial airbag and never need it than to need one and not have it.

Key take away from Chapter:

1. **Financial Protection is Essential** – Just like airbags, insurance policies provide crucial support during unexpected financial crises, ensuring stability and security.

2. **Rare but Life-Saving** – While accidents, illnesses, or disasters may not happen frequently, when they do, insurance can prevent devastating financial losses.

3. **Peace of Mind and Preparedness** – Having the right insurance policies allows individuals and families to focus on their lives without constant worry about future uncertainties.

4. **Not a Cost, but an Investment** – Many see insurance as an expense, but in reality, it is an

investment in financial security, much like installing airbags in a car.

5. **Timely Decisions Matter** – Just as airbags must be installed before an accident, insurance must be secured before a crisis. Delaying coverage can leave one vulnerable at the worst possible time.

"Invisible Shields, Priceless Safety"

Airbags of life, unseen but strong,

Protect us when things go wrong.

Silent they stay, in peace and light,

But rise like shields in a sudden fight.

Insurance stands like a hidden guard,

Life, health, and assets — it plays the card.

Rare it may be, but crucial the role,

A safety net for every life goal.

Ignore it not, or you may regret,

Airbags of wealth — secure and set.

CHAPTER 12

Diagnose Deficiency Through Annual Health & Wealth Check-up

Introduction

Just like a car requires regular servicing to perform optimally, both our health and wealth need periodic check-ups to identify deficiencies before they become serious problems. An annual health and wealth check-up ensures that we are on track for a long, secure, and prosperous life. Neglecting these check-ups can lead to irreversible consequences, affecting both our physical well-being and financial stability.

1. The Need for Regular Check-ups

Health Perspective

Many diseases, such as diabetes, hypertension, and certain cancers, develop silently without noticeable symptoms. Regular health check-ups can detect these conditions early, making treatment easier and more effective.

Wealth Perspective

Financial deficiencies—such as poor investment choices, insufficient savings, or lack of insurance coverage—can lead to financial stress, debt, or an insecure future. Regular wealth check-ups help individuals assess their financial health, adjust investment strategies, and plan for the future.

Imaginary Example

Ramesh, a 42-year-old executive, felt healthy and never visited a doctor for routine check-ups. One day, he fainted at work and was rushed to the hospital. He was diagnosed with high blood sugar and hypertension, conditions that had gone unnoticed for years. Similarly, he had never reviewed his investments and found out that inflation had eroded his savings. A timely health and wealth check-up could have prevented these shocks.

2. Components of an Annual Health Check-up

Basic Medical Tests

Blood Pressure & Sugar Levels: Identify hypertension and diabetes risk.

Cholesterol Check: Helps in assessing heart health.

Body Mass Index (BMI) & Obesity Test: To prevent lifestyle diseases.

Complete Blood Count (CBC): Detects infections and deficiencies.

Liver & Kidney Function Tests: Ensures vital organs are functioning well.

Cancer Screenings: Mammograms for women, prostate exams for men.

Lifestyle Assessment

Dietary Habits: Nutritional deficiencies can lead to serious health issues.

Exercise Routine: Lack of physical activity can result in obesity and cardiac problems.

Stress & Mental Health: Chronic stress affects both mental and physical health.

Imaginary Example

Neha, a 35-year-old marketing professional, went for her annual health check-up and discovered she had Vitamin D and iron deficiencies. With simple dietary changes and supplements, she improved her energy levels and overall well-being.

3. **Components of an Annual Wealth Check-up**

Review of Income & Expenses

Budget Analysis: Ensure you are saving at least 20-30% of your income.

Expense Audit: Identify unnecessary expenses and reallocate funds wisely.

Investment Portfolio Check-up

Equity & Debt Investments: Balance high-risk and low-risk assets.

Mutual Fund Performance: Compare returns with benchmarks and make changes if needed.

Retirement Planning: Ensure sufficient savings for post-retirement life.

Insurance Coverage Review

Health Insurance: Ensure coverage is sufficient for rising medical costs.

Life Insurance: Check whether your policy covers future family needs.

Home & Vehicle Insurance: Protect against unexpected damages or losses.

Tax Planning & Compliance

Tax Saving Investments: Utilize tax benefits under 80C, 80D, etc.

Filing Returns: Ensure timely and accurate tax filing to avoid penalties.

Imaginary Example

Amit, a 50-year-old businessman, realized during his annual wealth check-up that his life insurance coverage was outdated and insufficient for his family's needs. He upgraded his policies and also restructured his investments to generate better post-retirement income.

4. **Benefits of a Comprehensive Health & Wealth Check-up**

Early Detection of Problems – Identifying diseases or financial risks before they escalate.

Peace of Mind – Knowing that you are healthy and financially secure.

Informed Decision-Making – Making adjustments based on facts rather than assumptions.

Long-Term Well-being – A disciplined approach to both health and wealth ensures sustainability.

Improved Quality of Life – Less stress, better physical health, and financial freedom.

5. **Steps to Conduct Your Annual Health & Wealth Check-up**

Health Check-up Steps

Book an annual health check-up package.

Maintain a personal health record.

Discuss lifestyle changes with a doctor.

Act on any deficiencies detected.

Wealth Check-up Steps

Review financial statements and budget.

Check investment growth and returns.

Assess insurance policies and update as needed.

Set new financial goals for the year.

Imaginary Example

Vikas and his wife started doing annual health and wealth check-ups together. Over five years, they saw an improvement in their physical fitness and an increase in their net worth. Their friends, inspired by their disciplined approach, also adopted the habit.

Conclusion: Prevention is Better Than Cure

A stitch in time saves nine. Diagnosing deficiencies early—whether in health or wealth—ensures a smooth, stress-free life. Investing time in an annual check-up can protect against unforeseen crises and lead to a healthier, wealthier future.

Key take away from Chapter:

1. Health and wealth are interconnected—neglecting one affects the other.

2. Prevention is more cost-effective than cure.

3. Small lifestyle changes can make a big difference.

4. Regular financial assessments can help avoid future crises.

5. A disciplined approach leads to long-term well-being.

By making annual health and wealth check-ups a habit, we can live a more balanced and fulfilling life.

"Check to Protect, Year After Year"

Health and wealth, like a blooming tree,

Need care and checks to grow worry-free.

A silent flaw may hide deep inside,

Without a check, it's hard to decide.

Annual reviews keep troubles away,

Catching the cracks before they decay.

Health needs tests, wealth needs review,

Both need care to stay strong and true.

Don't wait for pain or a sudden fall,

Check-ups save — it's the smartest call!

CHAPTER 13

Starting Steps are Important to Reach Miles

Introduction

Success in life, whether personal or financial, begins with the first step. A journey of a thousand miles starts with a single step, and this principle applies to every goal—be it career growth, wealth accumulation, or personal development. The right beginning can set the tone for long-term success, while hesitation or an improper start can delay or derail progress.

In this note, we will explore the significance of strong initial steps in achieving major milestones. We will connect this concept to life goals, financial success, and real-world motivational examples that prove how early decisions shape the future.

1. Small Beginnings, Big Impact

The foundation of every great achievement is built on small but crucial first steps. Whether it is a new business, an investment portfolio, or a health transformation, the initial moves determine the trajectory.

Example: Dhirubhai Ambani – From Small Trades to Business Empire

Dhirubhai Ambani, the founder of Reliance Industries, started his journey by working in a small trading firm in Yemen. He returned to India with a vision and took small yet confident steps in textile manufacturing. Through disciplined financial planning, reinvestment of profits, and market expansion, he built one of the largest conglomerates in the world. His first steps in entrepreneurship laid the foundation for massive wealth creation.

Lesson: Bold and calculated first moves open doors to exponential growth.

2. Planning Before Action

While taking the first step is crucial, a well-thought-out plan amplifies success. Without direction, even the most enthusiastic beginning can lead nowhere.

Example: Sachin Tendulkar – Early Start with a Vision

Sachin Tendulkar's cricket career was not an accident; it was a result of early planning and disciplined training. From a young age, he practiced under his coach Ramakant Achrekar, followed a strict regimen, and focused on skill development. His early investment in practice helped him become one of the greatest cricketers.

Lesson: Preparation ensures that first steps are aligned with long-term goals.

3. Overcoming Initial Challenges

Many people hesitate to start due to fear of failure, lack of resources, or uncertainty. However, the ability to push through initial struggles defines long-term success.

Example: Warren Buffett – Investing from a Young Age

Warren Buffett started investing at the age of 11, making mistakes and learning from them. His initial setbacks did not discourage him; instead, he refined his strategies and built an empire in the stock market. His persistence in the early years made him one of the richest investors in history.

Lesson: The first few challenges are learning experiences that strengthen future success.

4. The Power of Consistency

Starting is important, but sustaining the momentum is equally critical. Initial efforts can only bear fruit if followed by consistent actions.

Example: Elon Musk – From Startups to Space Exploration

Elon Musk's journey from co-founding Zip2 to PayPal, Tesla, and SpaceX showcases how consistent innovation and perseverance lead to groundbreaking achievements. His early steps in software and online payments paved the way for ventures in electric cars and space technology.

Lesson: Momentum built in the early stages fuels long-term accomplishments.

5. Financial First Steps for Wealth Accumulation

Wealth creation is not an overnight phenomenon—it starts with small financial habits like budgeting, saving, and disciplined investing.

Example: A Common Middle-Class Investor

Consider a young professional who starts investing ₹5,000 per month in a systematic investment plan (SIP) from the age of 25. With consistent investing, compounding works its magic, and by retirement, the investment grows into a sizable corpus. However, if the same person delays investing by ten years, the final wealth accumulation is significantly lower.

Lesson: Small financial steps taken early can create substantial wealth over time.

6. Learning Before Earning

Many successful individuals emphasize the importance of acquiring knowledge before pursuing financial success.

Example: Ratan Tata – Learning Across Businesses

Ratan Tata worked in various Tata companies at the ground level before leading the Tata Group. His early exposure and learning experiences prepared him for major decisions like acquiring Jaguar-Land Rover and expanding globally.

Lesson: The right education and exposure in the early years lead to informed decision-making.

7. Importance of the Right Network

The people we surround ourselves with influence our success. Building the right connections early on can open doors to opportunities.

Example: Steve Jobs and Steve Wozniak – Building Apple Together

Apple was born because Steve Jobs and Steve Wozniak collaborated, combining technical expertise with business vision. Their early partnership played a crucial role in shaping Apple into a global technology leader.

Lesson: The right collaborations in the early stages accelerate growth.

8. Adapting and Pivoting After Initial Steps

Sometimes, the first step does not lead to immediate success, but the ability to adapt ensures eventual progress.

Example: Jeff Bezos – From Online Books to Global E-Commerce

Amazon started as an online bookstore, but Jeff Bezos quickly adapted to market needs and expanded into a global e-commerce giant. His ability to pivot after taking initial steps led to extraordinary success.

Lesson: The journey might evolve, but the willingness to start and adapt keeps progress on track.

9. Health and Wealth – Parallel Journeys

Just like wealth accumulation, good health also requires small but consistent efforts. The first steps towards a healthy lifestyle, like exercising or eating right, compound over time to yield long-term benefits.

Example: Virat Kohli – Transforming Through Fitness

Virat Kohli was not always the fittest cricketer, but he took conscious steps to improve his fitness, which ultimately transformed his game. His disciplined approach extended his career and made him a role model for young athletes.

Lesson: Small lifestyle changes early on lead to significant long-term benefits.

10. Taking Calculated Risks

Many people hesitate to take the first step due to fear. However, calculated risks often lead to the greatest rewards.

Example: Narayana Murthy – Quitting Job to Start Infosys

Narayana Murthy left a secure job to start Infosys with a small investment. His initial risk paid off, leading to the creation of one of India's biggest IT companies.

Lesson: Well-calculated risks in the beginning can yield extraordinary results.

Key take away from Chapter:

1. **Small beginnings lead to big successes** – Every great journey starts with a single, well-thought-out step.

2. **Consistency is key** – A strong start must be followed by continuous efforts.

3. **Early financial planning accelerates wealth accumulation** – The sooner you start saving and investing, the better.

4. **Adaptability ensures long-term success** – If the first step does not work, learn, pivot, and move forward.

5. **Taking calculated risks opens doors to opportunities** – Fear of failure should not stop progress.

Conclusion

Starting strong is crucial, but sustaining the journey with persistence, learning, and adaptability leads to long-term success. Whether it is building a career, accumulating wealth, or achieving personal growth, taking the right first steps ensures a rewarding journey ahead.

"Small Steps, Big Miles"

A journey to wealth starts small and slow,

Tiny steps today make fortunes grow.

Seeds of savings, though little they seem,

Can bloom into a financial dream.

First rupee saved is the first mile crossed,

Without a start, great wealth is lost.

Patience and time will pave the way,

But you must begin without delay.

Miles of fortune start with a stride,

Take that step — let success be your guide!

CHAPTER 14

Goodness & Faith Gives Satisfied Happy Life

Life is a journey filled with choices, actions, and consequences. The principles of goodness and faith play a vital role in shaping a satisfied and happy life. When connected with the philosophy of karma, ethical wealth accumulation, and unwavering belief in strategies, these virtues create a life of inner peace, prosperity, and long-term success.

1. Understanding Goodness and Faith

Goodness refers to moral integrity, kindness, and ethical behavior in all aspects of life. It is the foundation of positive karma, which eventually leads to success and fulfillment. Faith, on the other hand, is the trust in one's actions, principles, and strategies, even in challenging times. Faith provides the strength to keep moving forward and to stand by well-thought-out plans.

A satisfied and happy life is not just about financial success but about living with a sense of purpose and peace. People who act with goodness and maintain faith in the right path experience less stress, build strong relationships, and create lasting wealth in ethical ways.

2. The Role of Karma in a Happy Life

Karma is the universal law of cause and effect. Every action, thought, and decision has consequences. When one chooses goodness in dealings—whether personal or financial—it creates positive karma that brings happiness and success.

Helping others selflessly often results in unexpected support in return.

Ethical business practices lead to long-term trust and stability.

Investing with honesty and patience yields sustainable financial growth.

People who exploit others for short-term gains may accumulate wealth but often lose peace and happiness. Good karma, driven by ethical actions, ensures that wealth is not just accumulated but also brings joy and satisfaction.

3. Ethical Wealth Accumulation

Wealth, when acquired through honest and ethical means, becomes a source of peace rather than stress. The right way to accumulate wealth includes:

Hard work and continuous learning to enhance skills.

Fair business practices that ensure win-win situations for all stakeholders.

Long-term investments based on patience and sound financial strategies.

Giving back to society, which creates goodwill and inner fulfillment.

Many wealthy individuals who followed ethical paths—such as Warren Buffett or Ratan Tata—demonstrated that wealth acquired with integrity not only sustains but also brings deep satisfaction.

4. Keeping Faith in Strategies for Long-Term Success

Success in any area, including wealth accumulation, requires belief in well-planned strategies. Often, people abandon their plans due to temporary setbacks or failures. Faith in a sound financial strategy helps navigate market fluctuations, career uncertainties, and economic downturns.

Imagine an investor who has studied the market well and developed a diversified portfolio. If they panic during a market crash and sell everything, they lock in losses. However, if they have faith in their strategy, they stay invested and eventually see significant long-term growth.

Faith is not blind belief but trust built on knowledge, analysis, and experience. It allows individuals to stay committed to their goals, even when immediate results are not visible.

5. The Link Between Goodness, Faith, and a Happy Life

A person who upholds goodness and faith enjoys several benefits:

Peace of Mind: No fear of unethical repercussions.

Trust & Respect: Strong personal and professional relationships.

Financial Stability: Ethical wealth grows steadily over time.

Emotional Satisfaction: Knowing that one's actions create a positive impact.

Resilience in Tough Times: Faith provides inner strength during challenges.

6. Real-Life Examples of Goodness and Faith in Action

Case 1: The Honest Entrepreneur

A small business owner, Ramesh, always treated his customers and employees fairly. Even during financial difficulties, he never compromised on ethics. Over time, his business grew due to word-of-mouth trust, and he achieved long-term success. His wealth was not only financial but also in goodwill and happiness.

Case 2: The Investor with Faith

A young investor, Priya, followed a disciplined investment strategy. When the stock market crashed, many around her sold their holdings in panic. But she had faith in her strategy and stayed invested. Years later, her portfolio multiplied, while those who lost faith regretted their rushed decisions.

7. **Strengthening Faith Through Wisdom and Learning**

Faith is strengthened when backed by knowledge and wisdom. Ways to enhance faith in strategies and goodness include:

Studying and learning from successful individuals.

Seeking mentorship from experienced professionals.

Practicing patience and mindfulness.

Avoiding negative influences that create fear and doubt.

People who constantly educate themselves, seek advice from mentors, and remain committed to ethical values develop unshakable faith in their journey.

8. Challenges in Practicing Goodness and Faith

Despite their importance, goodness and faith are often tested in real life. Situations such as business losses, betrayals, and financial setbacks can shake one's belief. However, overcoming these challenges by staying true to principles is what leads to real happiness.

Overcoming Challenges:

Facing dishonesty from others: Respond with integrity and patience.

Financial losses: Learn from mistakes and stay committed to sound strategies.

Doubt from society: Stay focused on long-term goals rather than short-term approval.

Resilience in difficult times builds stronger character and deeper happiness.

Key take away from Chapter:

1. Goodness brings long-term success and inner peace. Ethical actions create positive karma that leads to sustainable happiness and wealth.

2. Faith in well-planned strategies ensures financial stability. Panic and doubt can derail success, while trust in the right path leads to long-term gains.

3. Wealth should be accumulated ethically to bring real satisfaction. Money earned through fair means brings peace, whereas unethical gains lead to stress.

4. Challenges test goodness and faith but should not break them. Staying true to principles even in tough times strengthens one's character.

5. Continuous learning and mentorship enhance faith. Seeking wisdom from mentors and life experiences builds strong decision-making and trust in one's journey.

By embracing goodness and maintaining faith in ethical strategies, one can lead a truly satisfied, happy, and prosperous life.

"Wealth with Goodness, Joy with Faith"

Gold may shine, but peace is rare,

Goodness and faith bring wealth with care.

A heart that gives and a mind that's true,

Attracts more fortune in all you do.

Money alone can't buy true delight,

But kindness and trust make futures bright.

Invest with honesty, share with grace,

Wealth grows faster in a happy place.

Faith in goodness is the ultimate key,

A satisfied life is true prosperity!

CHAPTER 15

Unnecessary Complications May Gives Stressful Life to Self and Family

In the pursuit of success, happiness, and wealth, many people unknowingly complicate their lives. The desire for "early and more"—be it in relationships, business, or investments—often leads to unnecessary stress and emotional turmoil. Instead of bringing peace and prosperity, such complications create conflicts, financial losses, and even health issues.

Let's explore how these unnecessary complications arise, their negative impact, and the benefits of avoiding them through a balanced and mindful approach.

1. The Burden of Unnecessary Complications in Life

Life is like a river; it should flow naturally. When people try to control every aspect, chase too much too soon, or interfere unnecessarily, they disrupt their own peace. Below are some key areas where unnecessary complications arise.

1.1 Relationships & Family Conflicts

Unrealistic expectations, ego clashes, and a desire to control everything often lead to broken relationships. Many families face unnecessary disputes because of competition, jealousy, or interference.

Example:

Amit and Rajesh were brothers who inherited their father's successful business. Amit, wanting quick expansion, took risky loans without consulting Rajesh. When the business faced losses, Rajesh blamed Amit, and their relationship turned bitter. Over time, their families stopped talking, and their once-loving bond was destroyed — all because of unnecessary haste and mismanagement.

1.2 Business & Work Stress

The corporate world rewards hard work, but many individuals complicate their professional lives by overloading themselves with responsibilities, engaging in unethical practices, or expanding too fast without proper planning.

Example:

Meena, a young entrepreneur, started an online clothing business. Within a year, she opened five more outlets without strengthening her supply chain. Managing multiple stores became overwhelming, quality dropped, and customers left. Instead of steady success, her impatience led to losses, debt, and extreme stress.

1.3 Investment & Wealth Mismanagement

Many people, in the greed for higher returns, put their money into complex financial products they don't understand. This not only leads to financial stress but also affects family security.

Example:

Suresh wanted to double his savings quickly. Ignoring safe investments, he put all his money into a high-risk cryptocurrency. When the market crashed, he lost everything. The financial burden led to arguments with his wife, mental stress, and insecurity about his family's future.

2. The Negative Aspects of Unnecessary Complications

When people complicate their lives unnecessarily, they invite stress, financial instability, and emotional suffering. Let's look at some key negative effects:

2.1 Emotional & Mental Stress

Constant worry about money, business, or relationships leads to anxiety and depression.

Fear of losing control makes people restless and impatient.

2.2 Broken Relationships & Loneliness

Family disputes over money, property, or control lead to isolation.

Friendships and partnerships break due to greed, ego, or miscommunication.

2.3 Financial Instability

Risky investments without proper knowledge result in massive losses.

Unnecessary spending to impress others leads to debt.

2.4 Health Issues

Stress from over-complication leads to high blood pressure, diabetes, and heart problems.

Lack of peace affects sleep, productivity, and overall well-being.

3. The Benefits of Avoiding Unnecessary Complications

A simple, balanced life brings happiness, stability, and peace. Let's see how one can benefit by avoiding unnecessary complications.

3.1 Stronger and Healthier Relationships

Open communication, trust, and realistic expectations create lasting bonds.

Avoiding unnecessary interference keeps family harmony intact.

3.2 Stress-Free and Peaceful Mindset

Focusing on essentials rather than chasing everything leads to mental peace.

Letting go of comparisons and unnecessary competition removes pressure.

3.3 Sustainable Business & Career Growth

Measured, planned decisions result in long-term success rather than short-term gains.

Ethical practices ensure credibility and steady progress.

3.4 Financial Stability & Wealth Creation

Investing in simple, reliable options secures the future.

Managing money wisely ensures long-term financial independence.

3.5 A Happier, More Fulfilling Life

Enjoying moments rather than being caught up in unnecessary struggles leads to true happiness.

A simple approach to life allows more time for loved ones and personal growth.

Key take away from Chapter:

1. **Simplicity brings peace** – Avoid overcomplicating life with unnecessary stressors.

2. **Balance is the key** – Moderation in expectations, money, and relationships prevents turmoil.

3. **Long-term vision wins** – Greed for quick success often leads to downfall.

4. **Clarity over complexity** – Choose simple, understandable financial and life choices.

5. **Happiness matters most** – A stress-free, content life is the ultimate success.

By eliminating unnecessary complications and focusing on what truly matters, one can create a life that is fulfilling, peaceful, and prosperous.

"Simplicity is Wealth's Best Friend"

Twisting investments like tangled thread,

Brings sleepless nights and growing dread.

Chasing quick gains or complex schemes,

Can turn your wealth into shattered dreams.

Simple plans with clear, steady pace,

Bring peace of mind and financial grace.

Why burden life with stress and strife?

Easy wealth paths lead to a stress-free life.

Keep it clear, keep it light,

Simple wealth grows strong and bright!

CHAPTER 16

Be Knowledgeable But Don't Swim in the Sea of Knowledge

Understanding the Demerits of Over-Knowledge and Overconfidence in Wealth Creation & Management

Introduction

Knowledge is a powerful tool that can guide individuals toward financial success. However, an excess of knowledge, if not applied wisely, can become a burden rather than a boon. Over-knowledge and overconfidence often lead to analysis paralysis, reckless decision-making, and financial losses. This note explores how too much information or excessive self-assurance can hinder wealth creation and management.

The Thin Line Between Knowledge and Over-Knowledge

Knowledge empowers individuals to make informed financial decisions, but over-knowledge can create confusion. With the explosion of financial content—books, courses, social media, and expert opinions—investors sometimes drown in a sea of conflicting advice.

Imaginary Example:

Raj, a young professional, started investing in stocks. Instead of following a simple strategy, he consumed excessive financial content daily, reading numerous books and listening to multiple experts. The conflicting views made him indecisive. One expert recommended real estate, another mutual funds, while yet another suggested cryptocurrencies. Paralyzed by too many choices, Raj kept switching investments, resulting in losses and missed opportunities.

Key Learning:

Being well-informed is essential, but excessive information without clarity leads to poor decision-making.

Overconfidence Can Lead to Financial Ruin

Overconfidence often stems from past successes, leading investors to believe they can outsmart the market or economy. Many individuals make wealth-destroying decisions based on an illusion of superior knowledge.

Imaginary Example:

Meena, a successful entrepreneur, made substantial profits in the stock market during a bull run. She believed she had mastered investing and started taking high-risk bets without analyzing market trends. When the market corrected, she lost a significant portion of her wealth, realizing that luck had played a big role in her earlier gains.

Key Learning:

A few wins do not make anyone an expert. The market is unpredictable, and humility is crucial in wealth management.

The Pitfalls of Ignoring Professional Advice

Some individuals, after acquiring financial knowledge, feel they no longer need expert advice. However, professionals bring experience and a structured approach that self-learners often lack.

Imaginary Example:

Amit, an IT professional, spent months studying personal finance. Convinced that he knew everything, he dismissed the idea of hiring a financial planner. Over time, he failed to account for tax implications, ignored asset diversification, and overlooked long-term planning. By the time he realized his mistakes, he had already lost a significant amount of wealth.

Key Learning:

Learning is good, but professional guidance adds depth and security to wealth management.

Over-Analysis Leads to Missed Opportunities

The urge to gather excessive knowledge often leads to decision paralysis, preventing individuals from taking timely action.

Imaginary Example:

Vikas wanted to invest in real estate. He researched various locations, mortgage rates, tax benefits, and market trends for years. By the time he decided, property prices had soared beyond his budget. His desire to make a "perfect" decision resulted in no decision at all.

Key Learning

Too much research without action can result in missed financial opportunities.

Simplicity Works Better Than Complexity

Many believe that complex financial strategies yield the best results. However, simple and time-tested approaches often outperform intricate methods.

Imaginary Example:

Nisha and Ravi both wanted to build wealth. Nisha followed a simple SIP investment plan, while Ravi experimented with options trading, high-risk derivatives, and advanced investment strategies. After a decade, Nisha's wealth grew steadily, while Ravi struggled with unpredictable gains and losses.

Key Learning:

A disciplined, simple investment approach is often more effective than over-complicating financial plans.

Conclusion

Financial knowledge is essential, but drowning in excessive information or becoming overconfident can be detrimental. Investors should seek balance — gaining knowledge but also applying it wisely without arrogance or hesitation.

Key take away from Chapter:

1. **Avoid Analysis Paralysis** – Too much information can lead to inaction; focus on practical application.

2. **Confidence Shouldn't Become Arrogance** – Past success doesn't guarantee future results; stay humble.

3. **Expert Advice is Valuable** – Professional financial planners provide structured guidance that self-learning may lack.

4. **Take Action at the Right Time** – Over-researching can lead to missed financial opportunities.

5. **Keep It Simple** – A straightforward, disciplined approach often yields better results than overcomplicated strategies.

By balancing knowledge with action and humility, one can achieve sustainable wealth without falling into the traps of over-analysis or overconfidence.

"Knowledge is Light, But Don't Drown in It"

Knowledge is gold, but too much can sink,

Diving too deep makes you overthink.

Markets will dance, rise and fall,

But wisdom is knowing — you can't know it all.

Too much advice may cloud your sight,

Simple steps often bring wealth's delight.

Learn, but act — don't just explore,

Or wealth will drift far from your shore.

Sail with knowledge, but don't lose your way,

Smart and steady wins wealth's bay!

CHAPTER 17

Give and Take – The Divine Rule of Nature and Wealth

Nature operates on a simple yet profound principle: give and take. The trees give oxygen and take carbon dioxide, rivers give water and receive minerals, and the sun gives warmth while absorbing energy from nuclear fusion. This divine rule of balance extends beyond nature into human life, relationships, and financial wealth.

In wealth management, understanding the principle of give and take is crucial. Those who only take without giving often find their wealth or success short-lived, while those who give wisely tend to create sustainable prosperity. This note explores how this rule applies to wealth creation, financial stability, and personal growth, with real and imaginary examples.

1. Nature's Lesson on Give and Take

Nature never functions on one-sided transactions. A seed absorbs nutrients from the soil, grows into a tree, and gives back fruits, oxygen, and shade. If a river stops giving water downstream, it stagnates and loses its purity.

Similarly, wealth should flow like a river. If someone hoards money without reinvesting or giving back to society, it becomes stagnant and loses value over time due to inflation, lack of circulation, or economic downturns.

Example: The Generous Farmer

A farmer who shares a portion of his high-quality seeds with neighbors ensures that the entire region has good crops. This prevents cross-pollination from inferior crops and guarantees his own farm's prosperity.

Likewise, businesses that share knowledge, train employees well, and invest in customer service create a thriving ecosystem that ensures long-term success.

2. Giving in Wealth Management – The Investment Mindset

Financial growth follows the give-and-take principle. Investors must give their money in the form of investments, stocks, or businesses to take profits. If they only hoard money in a locker, it neither multiplies nor contributes to economic growth.

Example: The Long-Term Investor

Warren Buffett, one of the world's richest men, follows this principle. He gives capital to undervalued businesses, nurtures them, and later takes substantial returns. His wealth compounds because he understands that giving (investing) strategically leads to taking (profits).

3. Giving Beyond Money – Time, Knowledge, and Value

Giving is not limited to money; it includes time, skills, and knowledge. Mentorship, networking, and sharing expertise often lead to unexpected wealth accumulation.

Example: The Tech Mentor

A software engineer spends time mentoring a junior developer without expecting anything in return. Years later, the junior developer builds a successful startup and offers the mentor a lucrative partnership.

This illustrates how giving knowledge and guidance can lead to wealth in unforeseen ways.

4. The Business Perspective – Giving Value to Gain Success

Successful businesses focus on giving value to customers before expecting profits. Companies that prioritize customer service, innovation, and ethical practices often dominate the market.

Example: The Coffee Chain's Strategy

A popular coffee brand introduces a 'Buy One, Give One' scheme, where for every coffee sold, one is given to the underprivileged. This social initiative increases brand loyalty, boosts sales, and ultimately grows the company's revenue.

This proves that strategic giving creates goodwill, customer trust, and long-term profits.

5. Charity and Philanthropy – The Secret to Sustained Wealth

Many billionaires, including Bill Gates and Ratan Tata, actively donate wealth, understanding that giving brings not just personal satisfaction but economic growth. Philanthropy often creates opportunities for wealth regeneration.

Example: The Charitable Businessman

A businessman donates to education funds, enabling thousands of students to study. Some of these students become successful and later invest back into his business or work for him, contributing to further wealth creation.

This cycle of giving and taking ensures prosperity for all involved.

6. The Myth of One-Sided Taking

People who only take without giving back eventually face setbacks. Businesses that exploit workers without rewarding them experience high attrition. Individuals who seek favors without reciprocating lose credibility.

Example: The Greedy Investor

A stock market investor only takes profits but never reinvests in companies during market downturns. Over time, the companies fail due to lack of investor support, and he loses his money too.

This highlights why taking without giving is unsustainable.

7. **Giving in Personal Finance – Savings and Generosity**

Just as one must invest to grow wealth, one must save to sustain financial security. Giving to one's future self in the form of savings, retirement funds, and emergency funds ensures that wealth remains stable.

Similarly, generosity—helping friends in need or supporting family—often results in goodwill and unexpected financial benefits.

Example: The Wise Saver

A middle-class man regularly saves and donates a small percentage of his income. During a crisis, his past generosity comes back as unexpected support from those he once helped.

This emphasizes the importance of balanced financial give-and-take.

8. Investing in People – The True Wealth

Wealth is not just about money; it's also about relationships. Giving time, respect, and kindness builds strong networks, which can be valuable in wealth creation.

Example: The Supportive Boss

A leader who mentors and supports employees earns their loyalty. Years later, when he starts his own business, these employees join him, helping him build a successful enterprise.

This proves that investing in people brings long-term rewards.

9. The Spiritual Perspective – Giving Attracts Prosperity

Many spiritual traditions emphasize that giving increases prosperity. Acts of kindness, charity, and fair business practices often bring positive energy and financial stability.

Example: The Businessman Who Shared

A merchant known for fair trade and generous donations always finds his business thriving, despite market fluctuations. His goodwill ensures customer loyalty and financial success.

This supports the belief that ethical wealth practices lead to sustained prosperity.

10. Striking a Balance – When to Give and When to Take

Giving without discernment can lead to depletion, while taking without balance leads to loss. Understanding when and how much to give or take is crucial.

Example: The Over-Giver

A person who constantly lends money without expecting repayment eventually struggles financially. However, when he learns to give wisely—investing in productive ventures instead of reckless loans—he finds stability.

This highlights the importance of strategic giving.

Key take away from Chapter:

1. **Wealth Should Flow Like a River** – Hoarding money stagnates wealth, while strategic investments and generosity create long-term financial health.

2. **Giving Brings Unexpected Returns** – Helping others, mentoring, or donating often leads to unanticipated financial or social benefits.

3. **Balance is Crucial** – Over-giving without strategy leads to loss, while one-sided taking leads to failure.

4. **Invest in People and Relationships** – Supporting others builds strong networks that contribute to wealth accumulation.

5. **Ethical Giving Leads to Prosperity** – Fair trade, charity, and value-driven business practices ensure sustained financial success.

Conclusion

The divine rule of give and take is evident in nature, personal life, and wealth management. Those who give wisely — whether money, time, or knowledge — often receive far more in return. Whether through investments, philanthropy, or ethical business practices, embracing this principle is the key to lasting prosperity.

By aligning financial strategies with this rule, individuals and businesses can create a cycle of wealth that benefits not just themselves but society as a whole.

"Give and Take — Wealth's Natural Flow"

The river flows and fills the sea,

Yet rain returns, as nature's decree.

Wealth works the same — give and you'll gain,

Hold it too tight, and you'll feel the strain.

Share your riches, let kindness flow,

Prosperity blooms where good deeds grow.

Give to grow, take with grace,

This divine rule keeps wealth in place.

The more you give, the more you make,

Nature's secret — **Give and Take!**

CHAPTER 18

Enjoy Fruits in Life Before They Rot: Smart Wealth Usage for Lifestyle Improvement

Wealth accumulation is a significant achievement, but it is only one part of financial success. The true essence of wealth lies in using it wisely to improve lifestyle, create meaningful experiences, and ensure well-being. Just as fruits must be enjoyed before they rot, wealth should be utilized effectively to bring joy, comfort, and security before time diminishes its value.

1. Understanding the Balance Between Wealth Accumulation and Enjoyment

Many people dedicate their entire lives to accumulating wealth but fail to enjoy it. Some hoard their riches, always waiting for the "perfect time" to indulge in luxury, travel, or experiences. However, excessive frugality can lead to a life of missed opportunities, where money remains unused and eventually loses its true purpose.

Conversely, some people squander their wealth on unnecessary extravagance, leaving themselves vulnerable in times of need. The key lies in balancing financial discipline with a well-planned approach to lifestyle improvement.

2. The Value of Wealth in Enhancing Life's Quality

Wealth provides the means to elevate one's quality of life in various ways:

Better Health: Investing in preventive healthcare, a nutritious diet, and fitness programs ensures a long and active life.

Luxury and Comfort: Living in a comfortable home, driving a reliable vehicle, and experiencing occasional luxury can enhance day-to-day life.

Travel and Exploration: Exploring different cultures, places, and cuisines enriches one's perspective and brings lifelong memories.

Education and Self-Growth: Continuous learning, acquiring new skills, and attending insightful seminars or workshops contribute to personal and professional growth.

Charitable Giving: Sharing wealth with those in need or contributing to causes creates a legacy of kindness and positive impact.

3. The Risk of Delayed Enjoyment

Delaying lifestyle improvements indefinitely can lead to:

Health Decline: People who wait too long to take care of their health may suffer from illnesses that prevent them from fully enjoying their wealth later in life.

Missed Experiences: Some opportunities, like traveling with young children, require timely action. Once gone, they may never return.

Depreciation of Wealth's Value: Money that sits idle loses value due to inflation, whereas invested in meaningful experiences, it creates lasting joy.

Imaginary Example 1: Rajesh's Cautionary Tale

Rajesh, a successful businessman, worked tirelessly for 35 years, saving and investing every penny. He postponed vacations, ignored health concerns, and avoided spending on luxuries, always telling himself he would enjoy life after retirement. However, at 65, health issues limited his ability to travel, and his children had grown distant. He had the wealth but not the time or health to enjoy it.

4. **Enjoying Wealth Without Compromising Financial Security**

Spending should be structured to ensure both enjoyment and financial stability. The following strategies can help:

A. Setting Lifestyle Enhancement Goals

Allocate a portion of wealth for travel, hobbies, and experiences.

Upgrade housing and living standards within reasonable financial limits.

Plan for health and well-being, including quality healthcare and fitness programs.

B. Using the 50-30-20 Rule for Balanced Spending

A well-structured wealth utilization plan can be:

50% for needs (housing, health, daily expenses).

30% for wants (luxuries, travel, hobbies).

20% for future security (investments, emergency funds, and retirement).

Imaginary Example 2: Meera's Balanced Approach

Meera, a corporate professional, divided her wealth into different categories. She regularly traveled, indulged in fine dining occasionally, and upgraded her home for comfort. At the same time, she maintained savings and investments, ensuring her financial future remained secure. This approach allowed her to enjoy life while keeping her wealth intact.

5. The Importance of Timely Wealth Usage

A. Investing in Meaningful Experiences

Using wealth to create lasting memories through travel, learning, and family bonding is more valuable than simply accumulating material possessions.

B. Prioritizing Health and Wellness

Investing in health early on ensures a longer, healthier life where wealth can be truly enjoyed.

C. Smart Philanthropy for a Fulfilling Life

Giving back to society not only helps others but also brings immense personal satisfaction.

Imaginary Example 3: Arjun's Generous Legacy

Arjun, a retired entrepreneur, ensured his wealth benefited both his family and society. He funded education for underprivileged students, supported medical research, and traveled the world with his wife. By doing so, he maximized his wealth's impact rather than letting it sit idle.

6. Avoiding Overindulgence: Responsible Enjoyment of Wealth

While enjoying wealth is essential, excessive indulgence can lead to financial distress. Some common mistakes include:

Overspending on depreciating assets like luxury cars and gadgets.

Ignoring long-term financial security while focusing only on present pleasures.

Succumbing to lifestyle inflation, where increased income leads to unnecessary expenditure.

Imaginary Example 4: Vikram's Costly Mistake

Vikram inherited a large fortune but spent recklessly on luxury cars, parties, and unnecessary extravagances. Within a decade, his wealth had dwindled, leaving him struggling financially. His story highlights the importance of moderation and planning.

7. **Creating a Sustainable Wealth Utilization Plan**

To ensure a lifetime of financial security while enjoying the benefits of wealth, consider:

Regularly Reviewing Financial Plans: Adjust spending as per evolving goals and priorities.

Investing in Income-Generating Assets: Real estate, stocks, and businesses can provide continued wealth growth.

Passing Down Wealth Wisely: Planning inheritance and legacy to benefit future generations.

Key take away from Chapter:

1. **Balance is Essential**: Wealth should be enjoyed responsibly, ensuring both present pleasure and future security.

2. **Health is the True Wealth**: Using money to maintain good health ensures a fulfilling life.

3. **Experiences Matter More than Possessions**: Travel, learning, and family bonding provide lifelong happiness.

4. **Plan for the Future While Living in the Present**: A well-structured financial plan allows enjoyment without jeopardizing security.

5. **Give Back to Society**: Wealth is most meaningful when it positively impacts others.

Conclusion

Money is a tool, not the ultimate goal. Just as fruits must be consumed before they rot, wealth should be utilized to enhance life rather than being hoarded indefinitely. A well-balanced approach ensures that wealth serves its true purpose—bringing joy, comfort, and a legacy of fulfillment.

"Taste the Fruits Before They Rot"

Wealth like fruits, ripens with time,

Use it wisely — it's truly prime.

Save and grow, but don't just store,

Enjoy your life, there's so much more!

Money unused is like fruit left to waste,

Enjoy its sweetness with joy and taste.

Travel, explore, fulfill your dream,

Let your wealth add life's true gleam.

Before time withers what you've got,

Enjoy your fruits — before they rot!

End Note

Dear Reader,

We sincerely thank you for investing your valuable time in reading this book. Through the chapters, we have drawn parallels between nature's wisdom and the principles of wealth creation, management, and utilization. Just as nature operates on balance, patience, and sustainability, so does wealth when handled with the right mindset and discipline.

We hope this book has provided you with meaningful insights to help you build, protect, and enjoy your wealth while ensuring a stable and fulfilling life. Whether it is about sowing the right seeds of investment, preparing for uncertainties, or embracing the cycle of financial growth, each chapter is designed to inspire you to make informed and wise financial choices.

Remember, wealth is not just about accumulation—it is about purposeful utilization, securing the future, and contributing to the well-being of those around us. Let the lessons from nature guide you in your financial journey, just as they have guided humanity for centuries.

If you found this book informative and a helpful guide in wealth management, we encourage you to share its wisdom. **Refer this book to at least 10 of your near and dear ones**. In doing so, you will not only contribute to their financial well-being but also create a positive ripple effect in your community.

We wish you prosperity, wisdom, and a life enriched with both financial and personal abundance.

Happy Wealth Creation!

– Harish Kalra

(The Author)

Disclaimers

1. **Stock Market Disclaimer**

    Investing in the stock market is subject to market risks. The value of stocks may fluctuate based on market conditions, economic factors, and company performance. Past performance is not indicative of future results. Readers are advised to conduct their own research, seek professional financial advice, and carefully assess their risk tolerance before investing. The authors and publishers are not responsible for any financial loss incurred based on the strategies or suggestions mentioned in this book.

2. **Mutual Fund Disclaimer**

    Mutual fund investments are subject to market risks, Please read all scheme-related documents carefully before investing. The performance of a mutual fund is not guaranteed, and NAVs (Net Asset Values) may go up or down depending on market conditions. This book does not endorse any specific mutual fund or investment product. Readers should consult with a financial advisor before making any investment decisions.

3. Insurance Disclaimer

Insurance policies are subject to terms, conditions, exclusions, and eligibility criteria as set by the respective insurance providers and regulatory authorities. This book provides general information on insurance as a financial protection tool and does not constitute an offer, solicitation, or recommendation of any specific insurance product. Readers should carefully review the policy documents and consult a qualified insurance advisor before purchasing any insurance product.

4. General Disclaimer

The information provided in this book is for educational and informational purposes only and should not be considered as financial, legal, tax, or investment advice. The authors and publishers have made efforts to ensure accuracy but do not guarantee the completeness or reliability of the content. Readers are encouraged to consult certified professionals before making any financial decisions. The authors and publishers are not liable for any financial or non-financial losses resulting from the application of concepts discussed in this book.

By reading this book, you acknowledge and agree to the above disclaimers.

www.ingramcontent.com/pod-product-compliance
Lightning Source LLC
Chambersburg PA
CBHW062140150726
47991CB00006B/2120